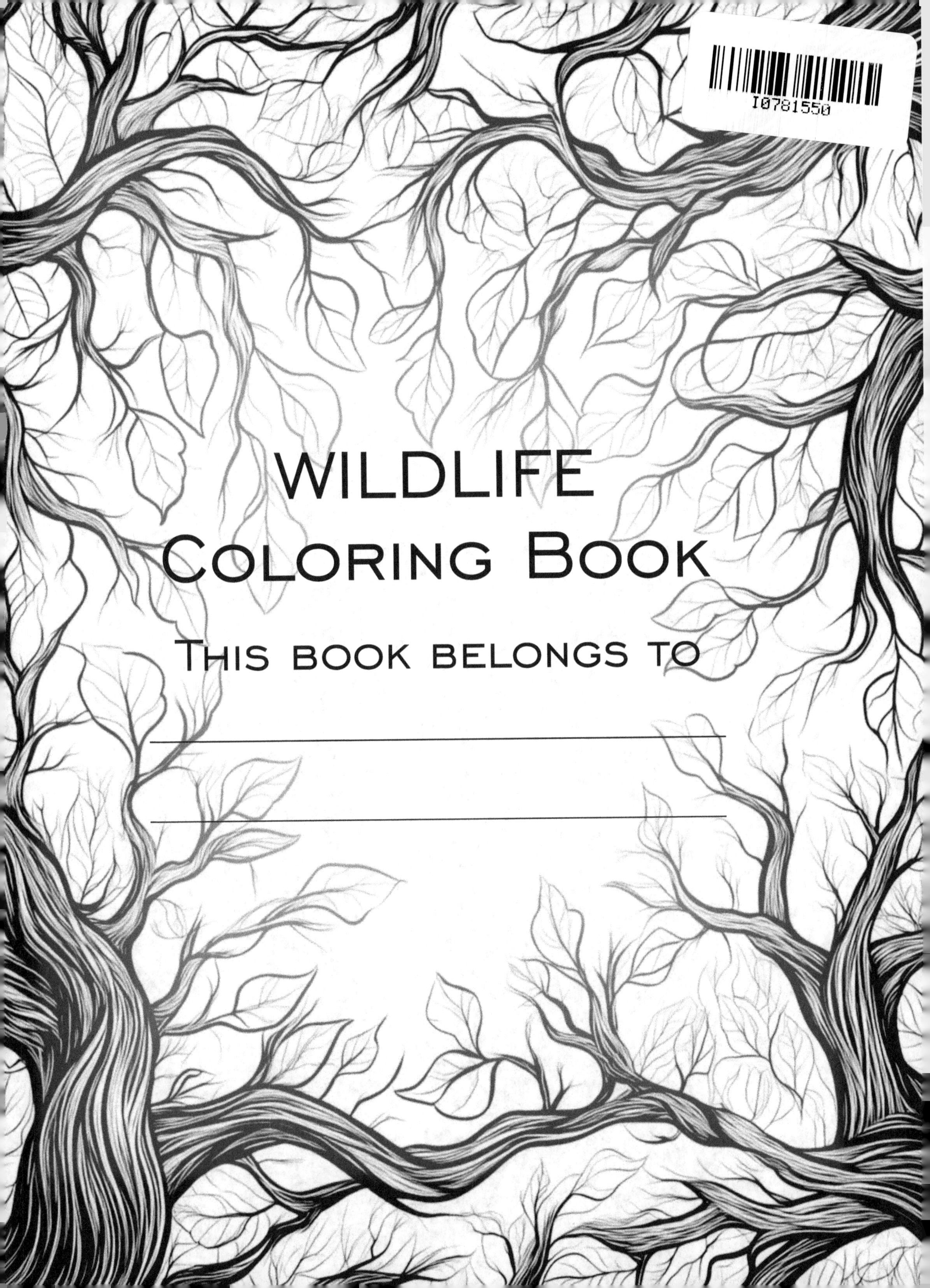

WILDLIFE
Coloring Book

This book belongs to

____

____

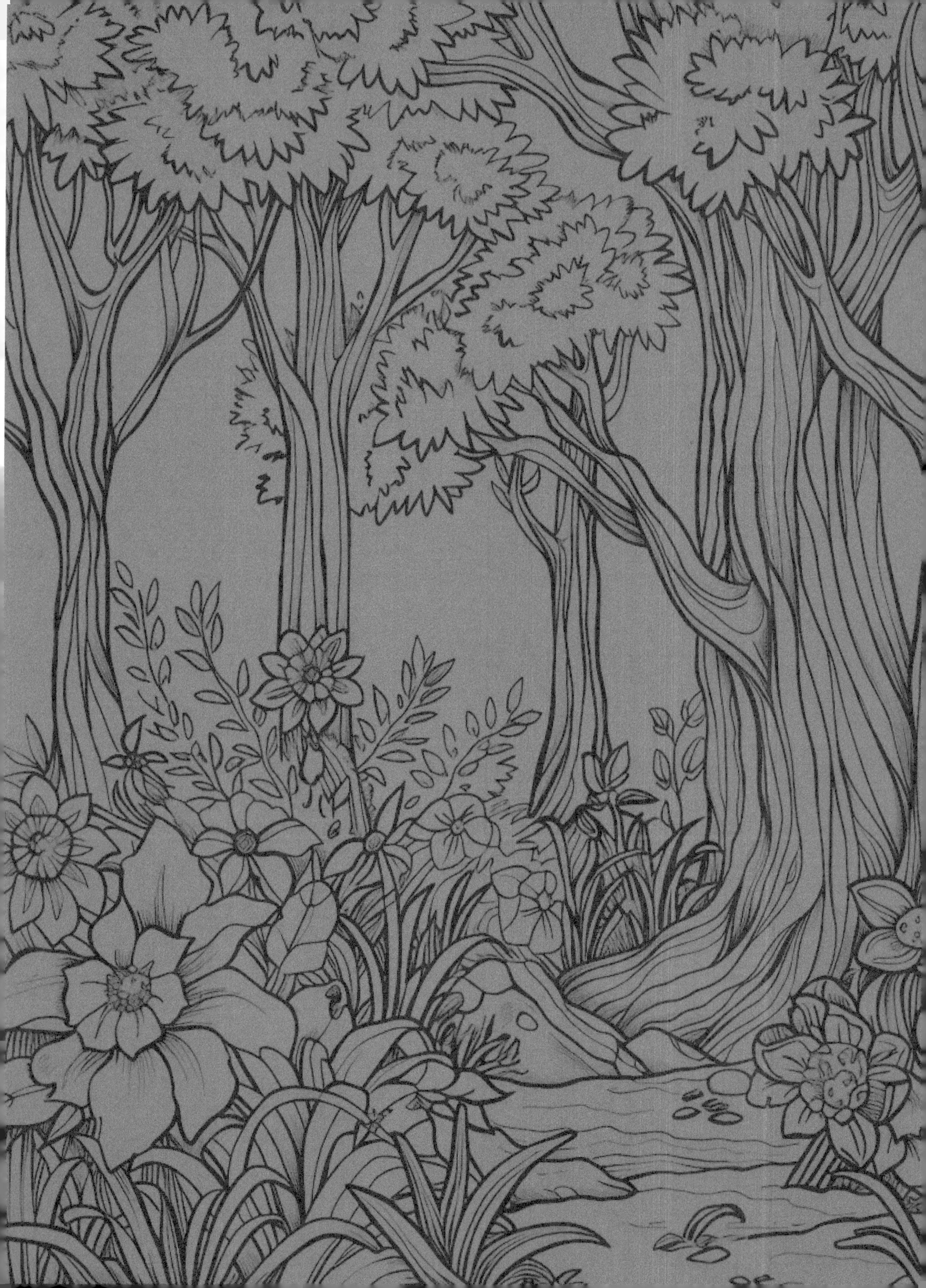

COLOR TEST PAGE

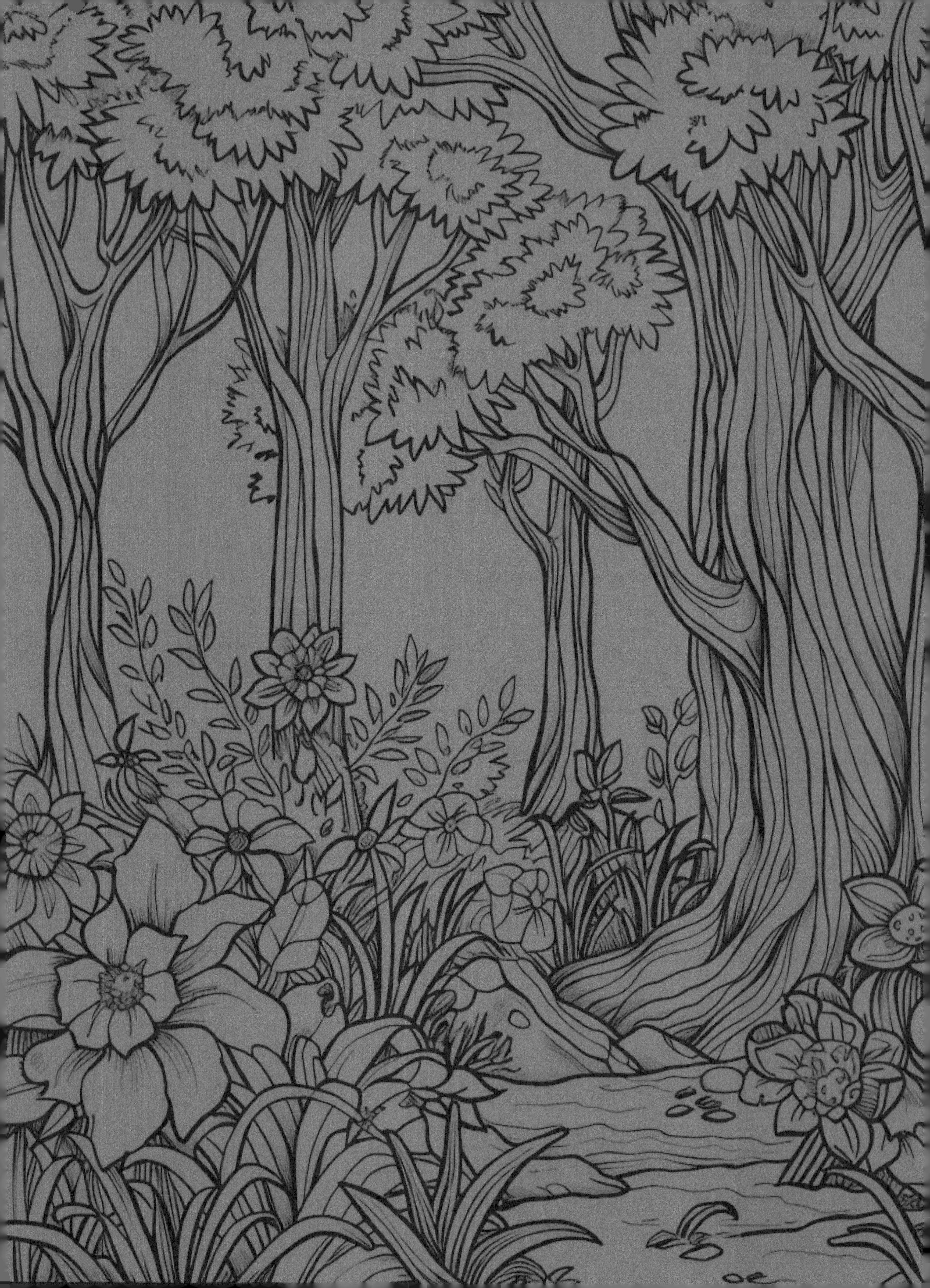

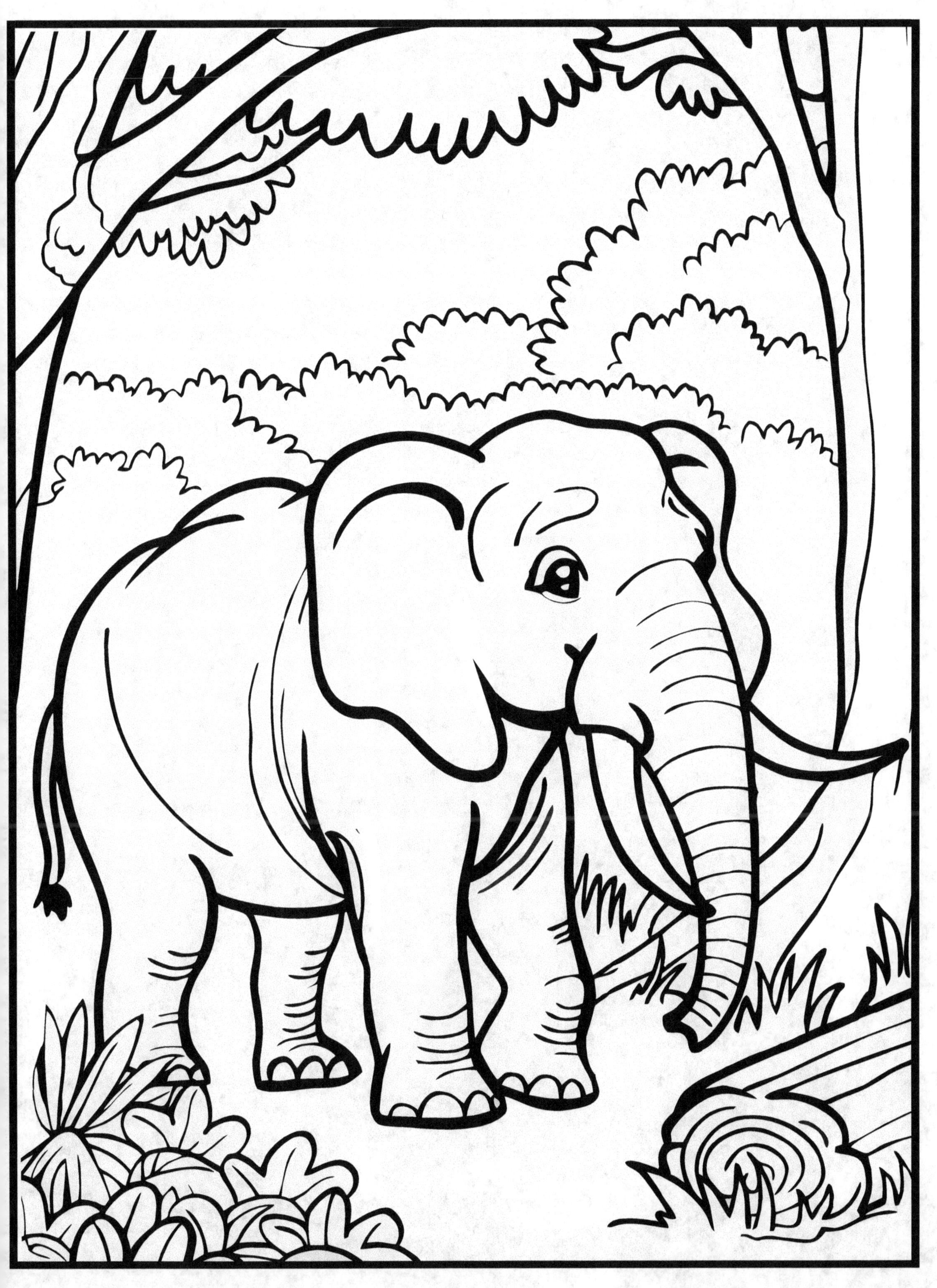

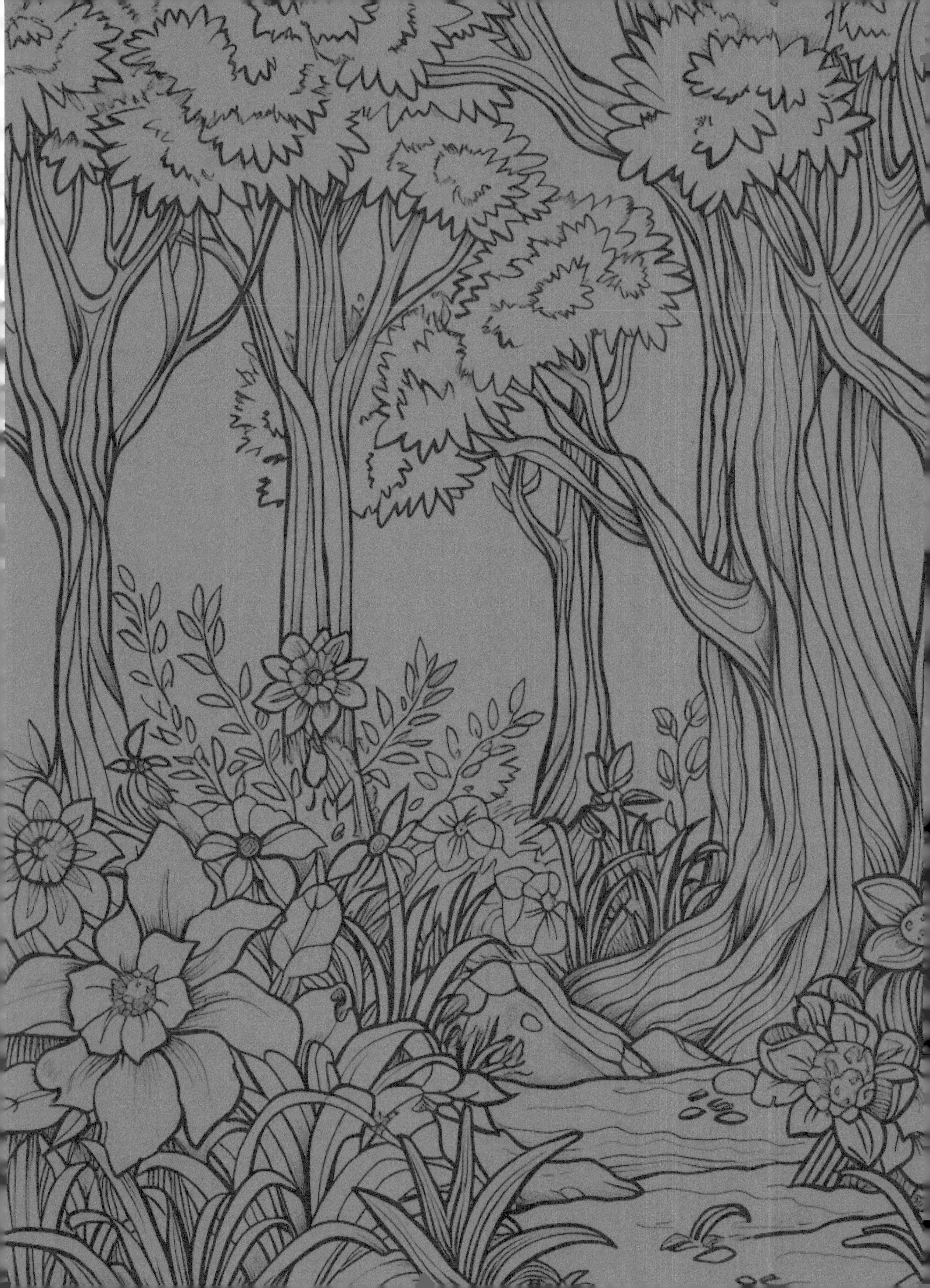

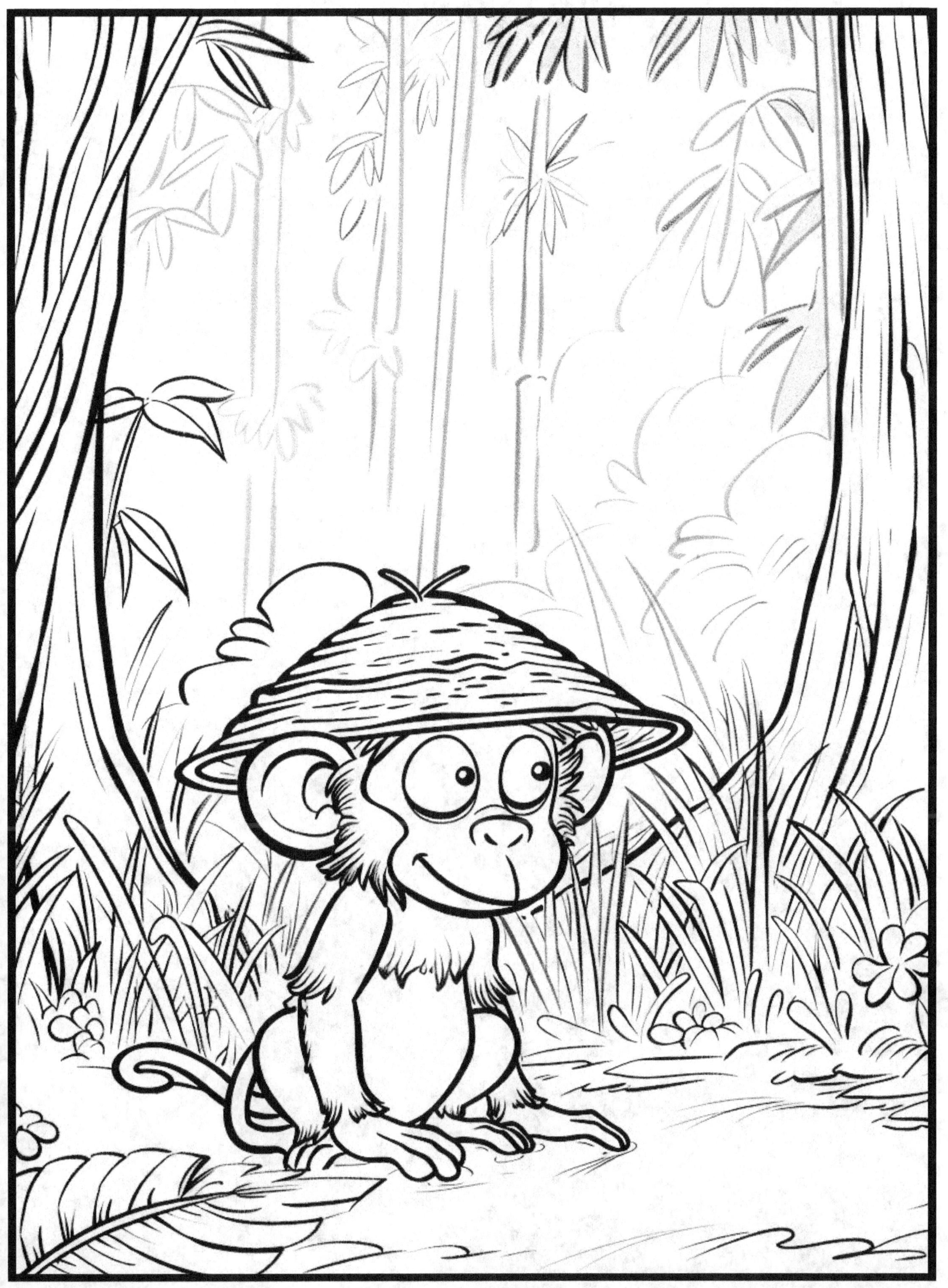

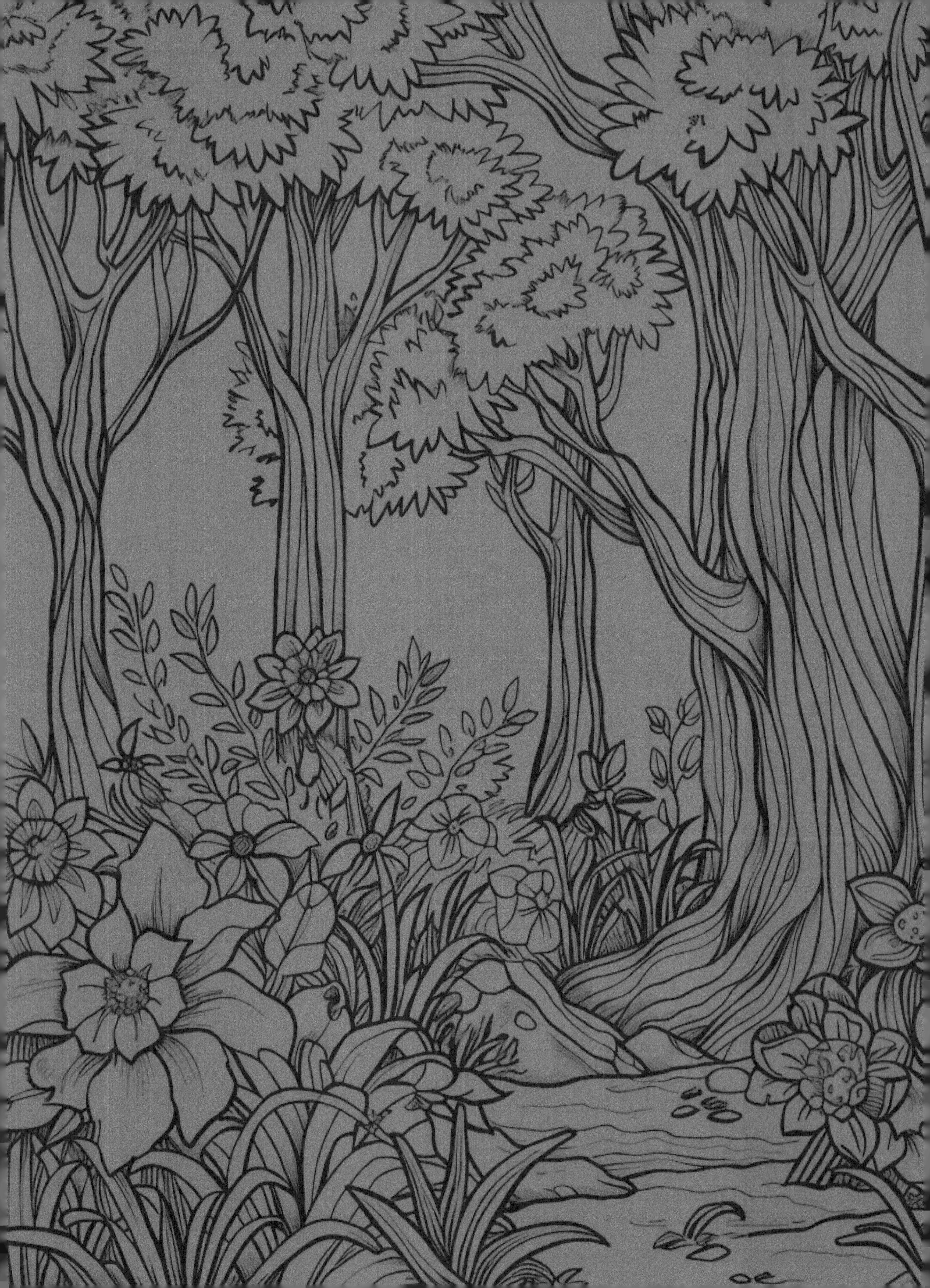

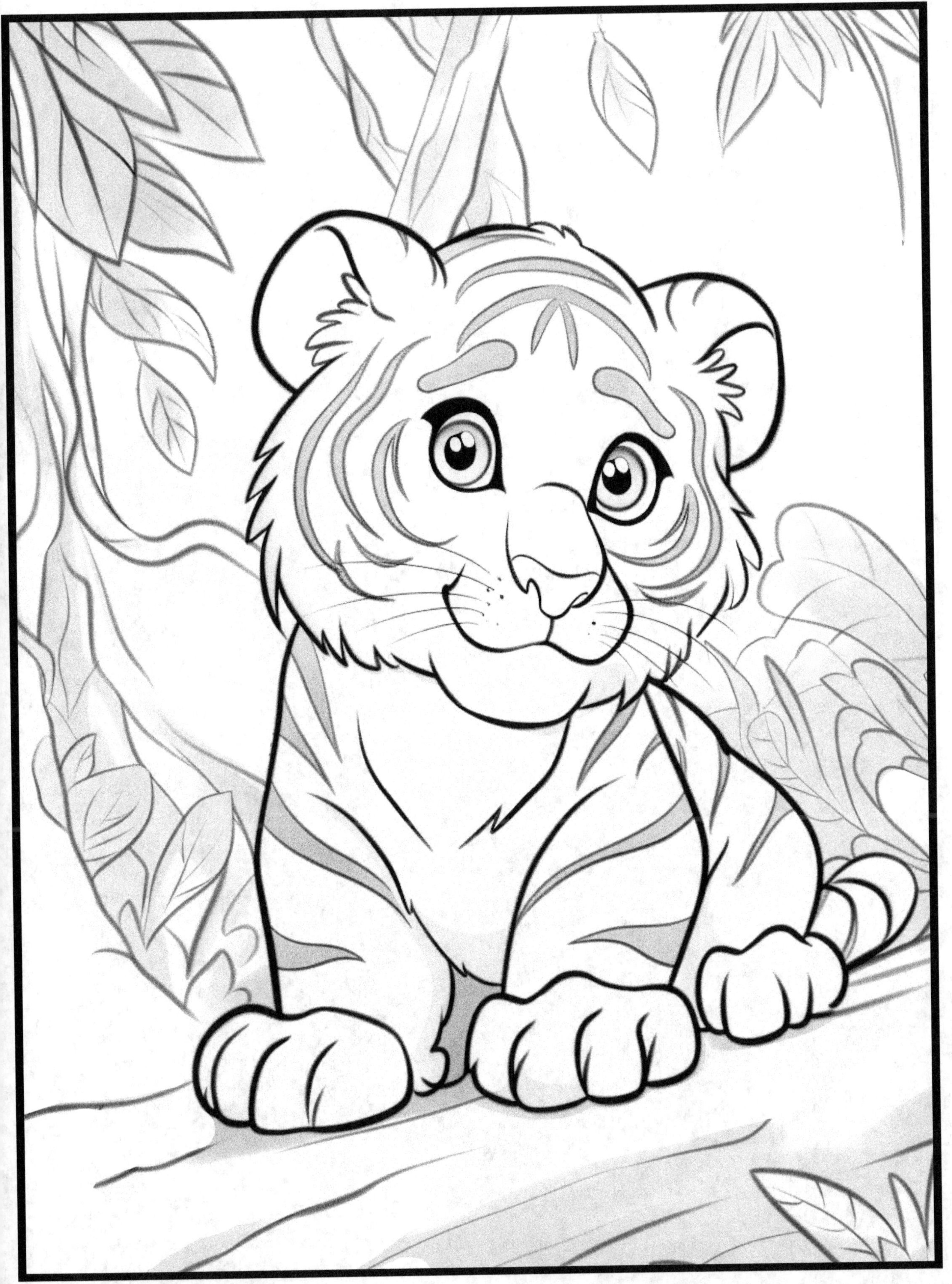

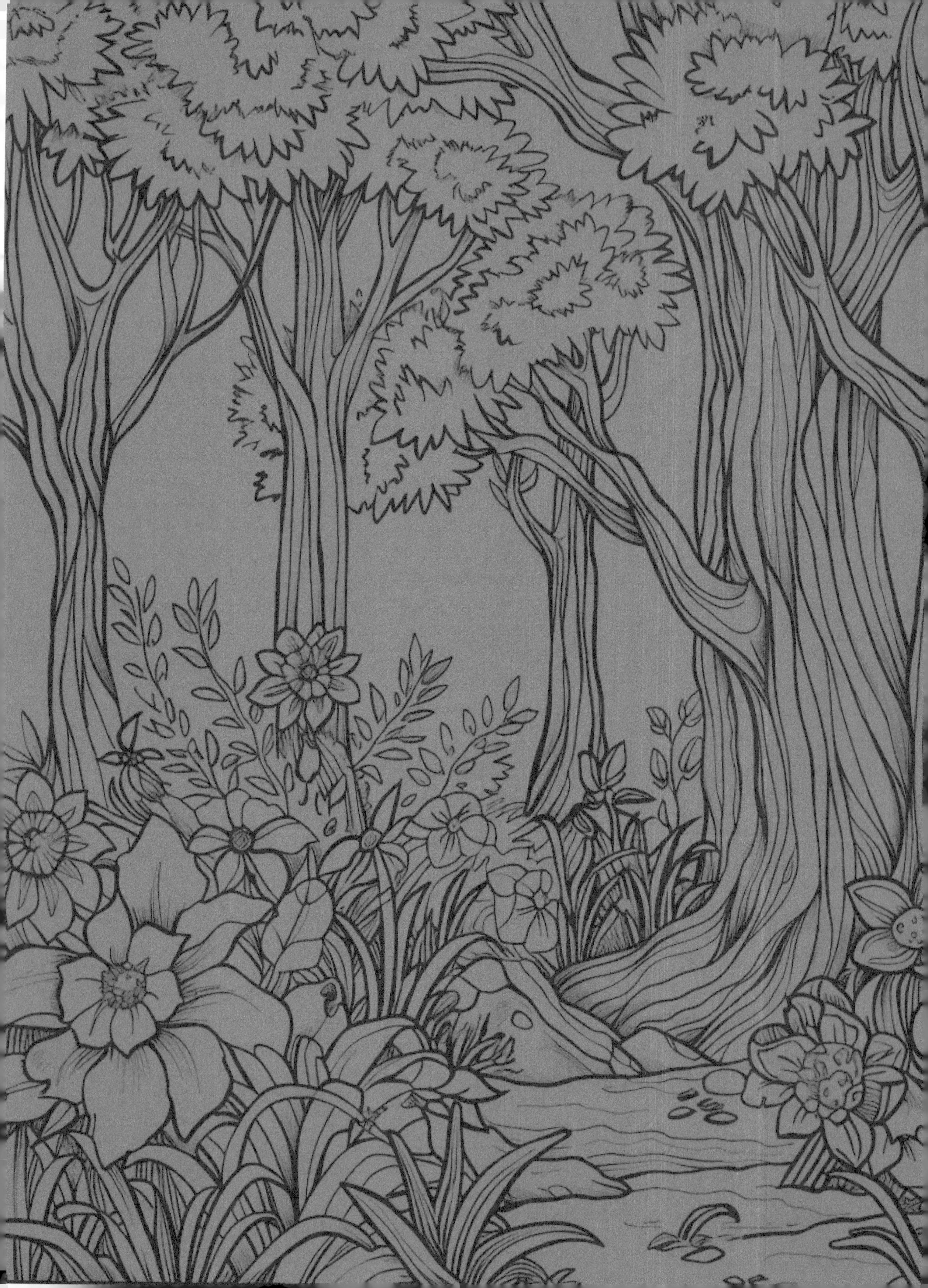

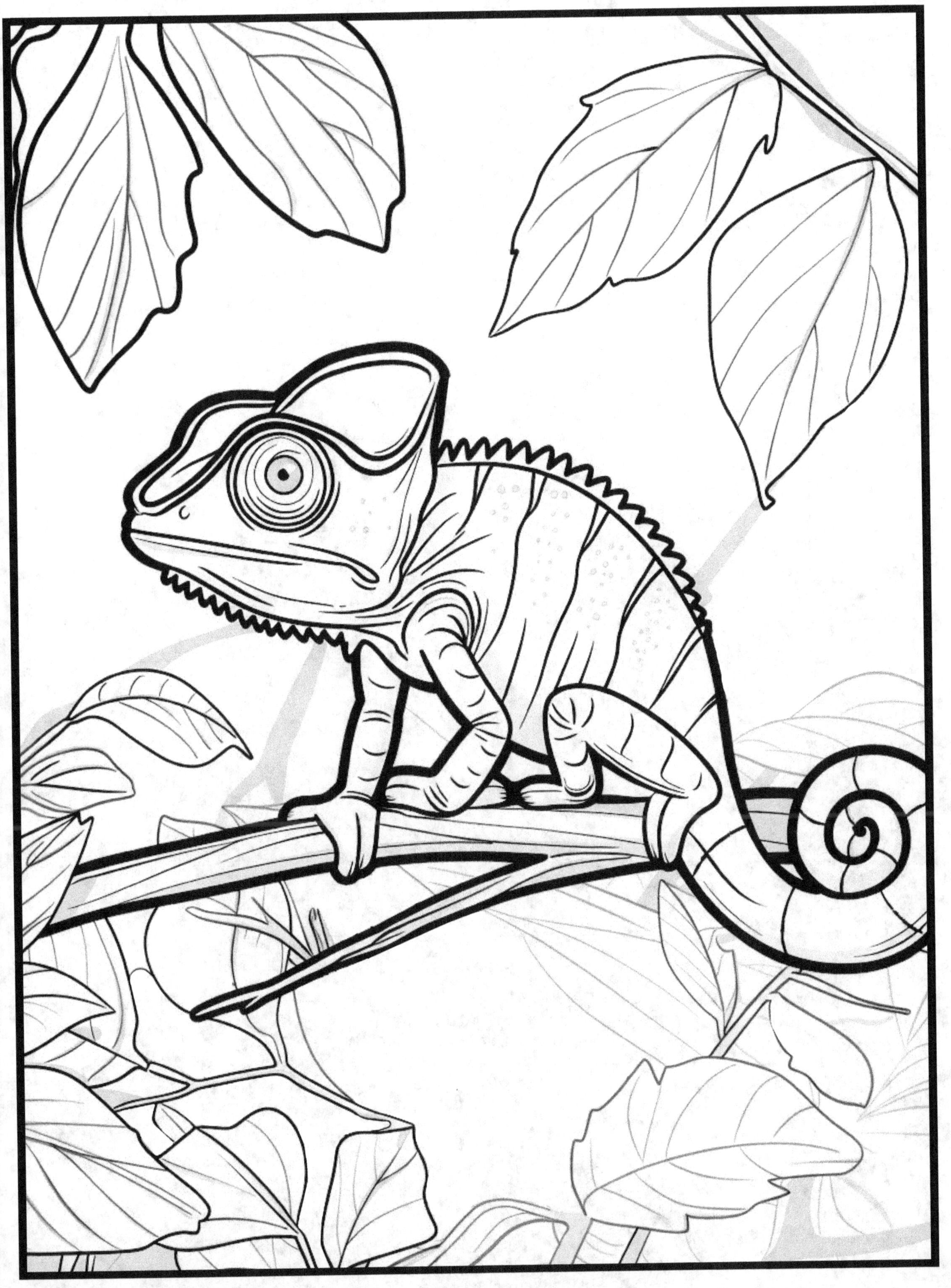

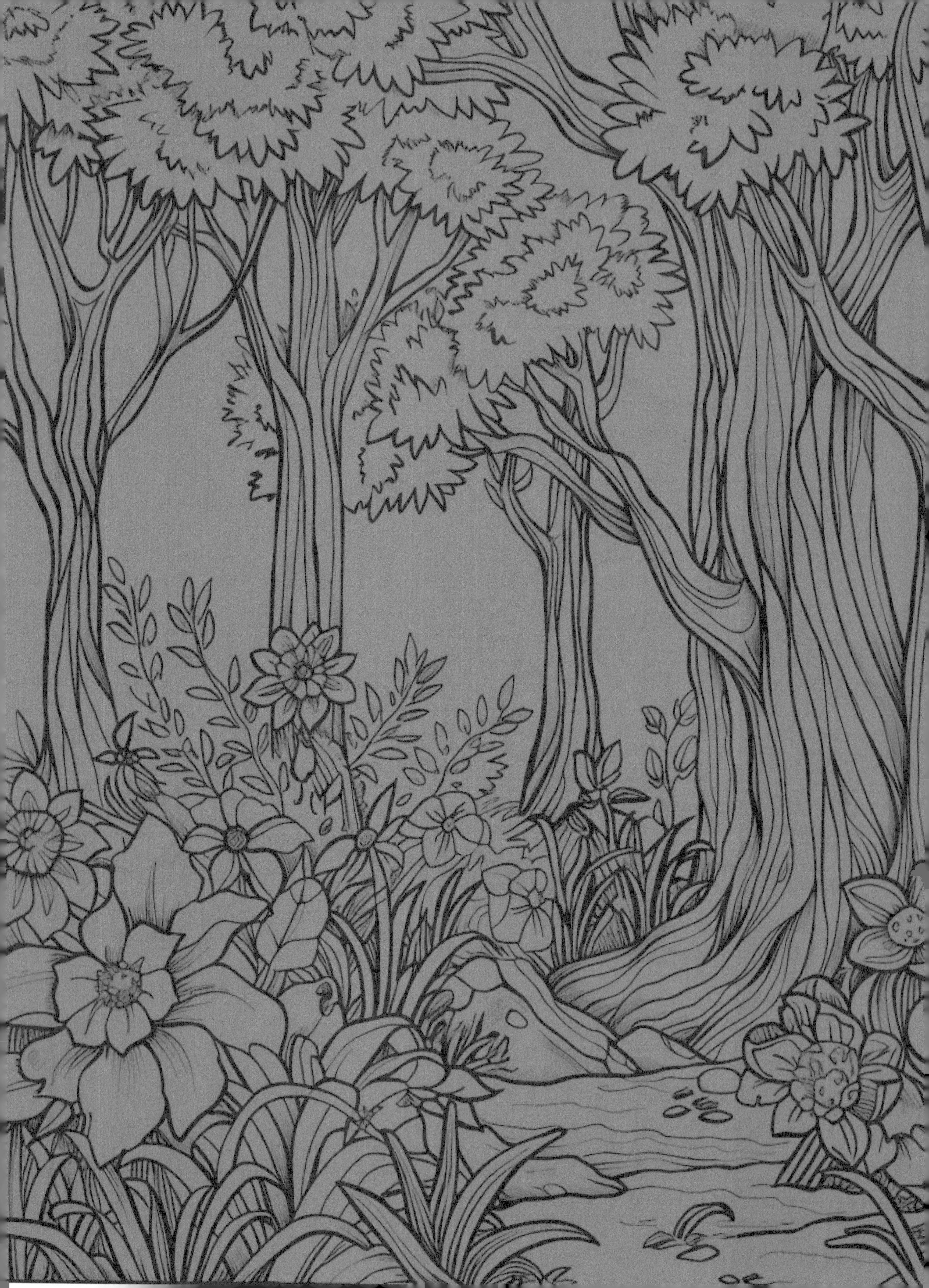

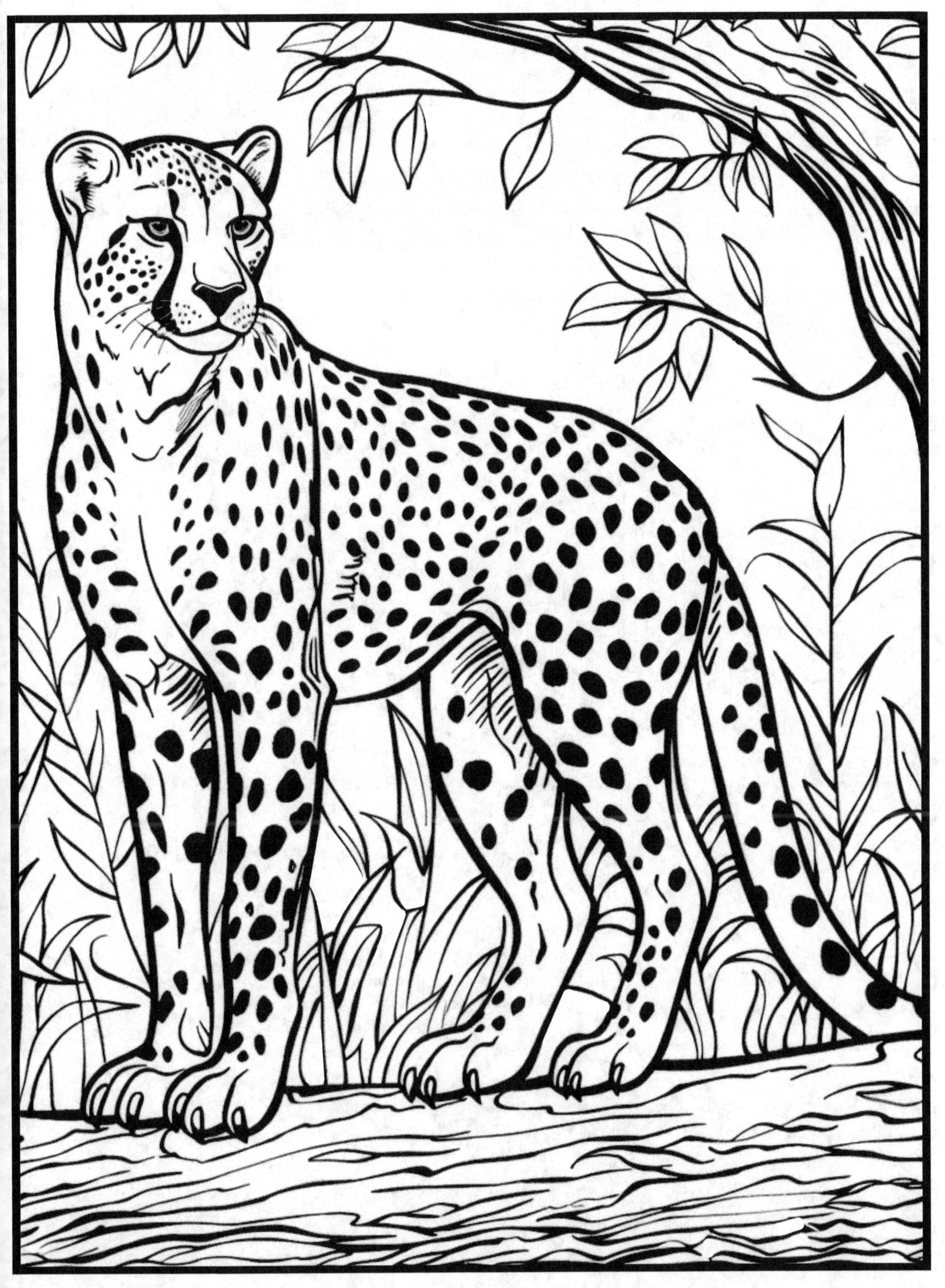

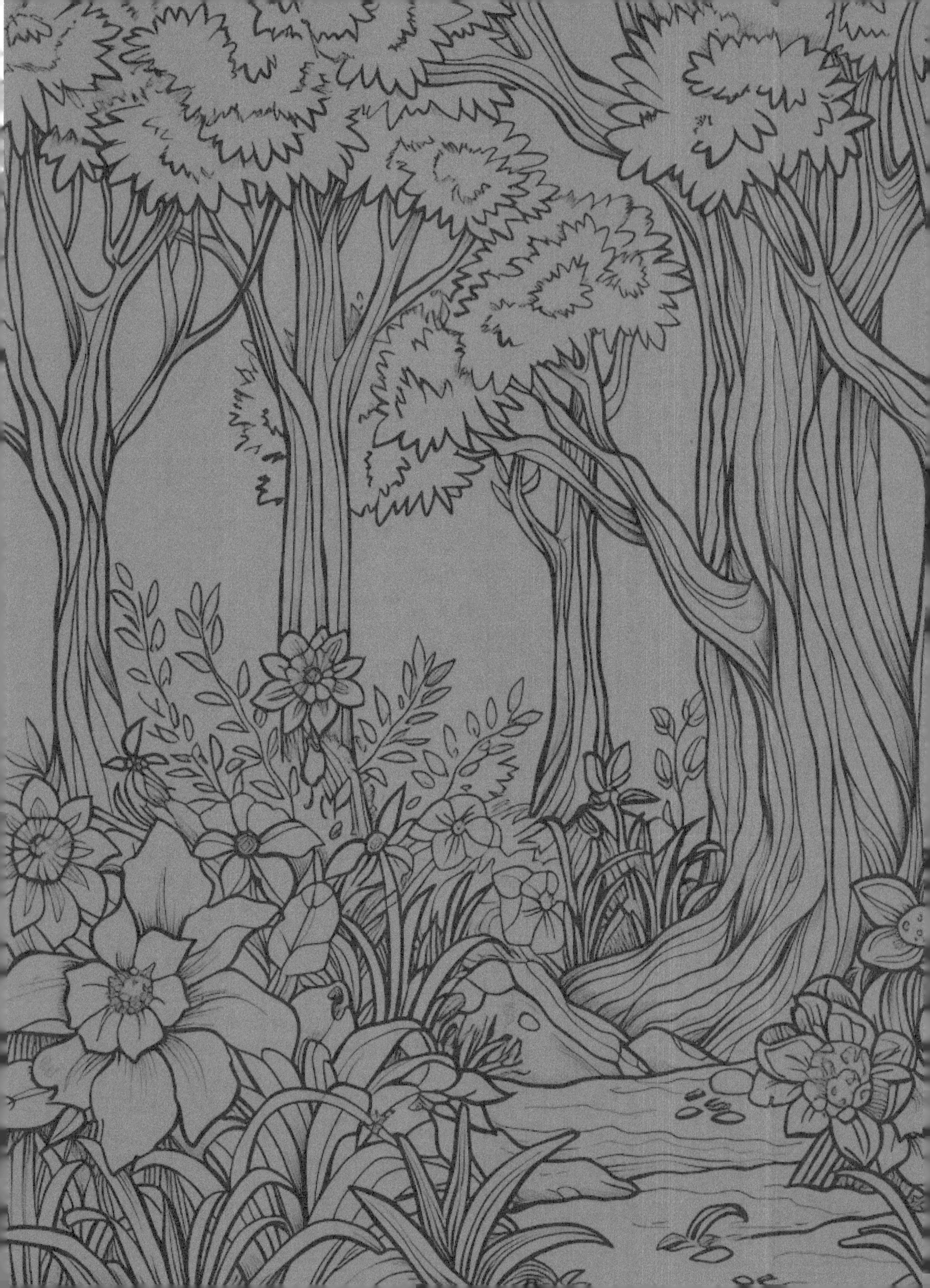

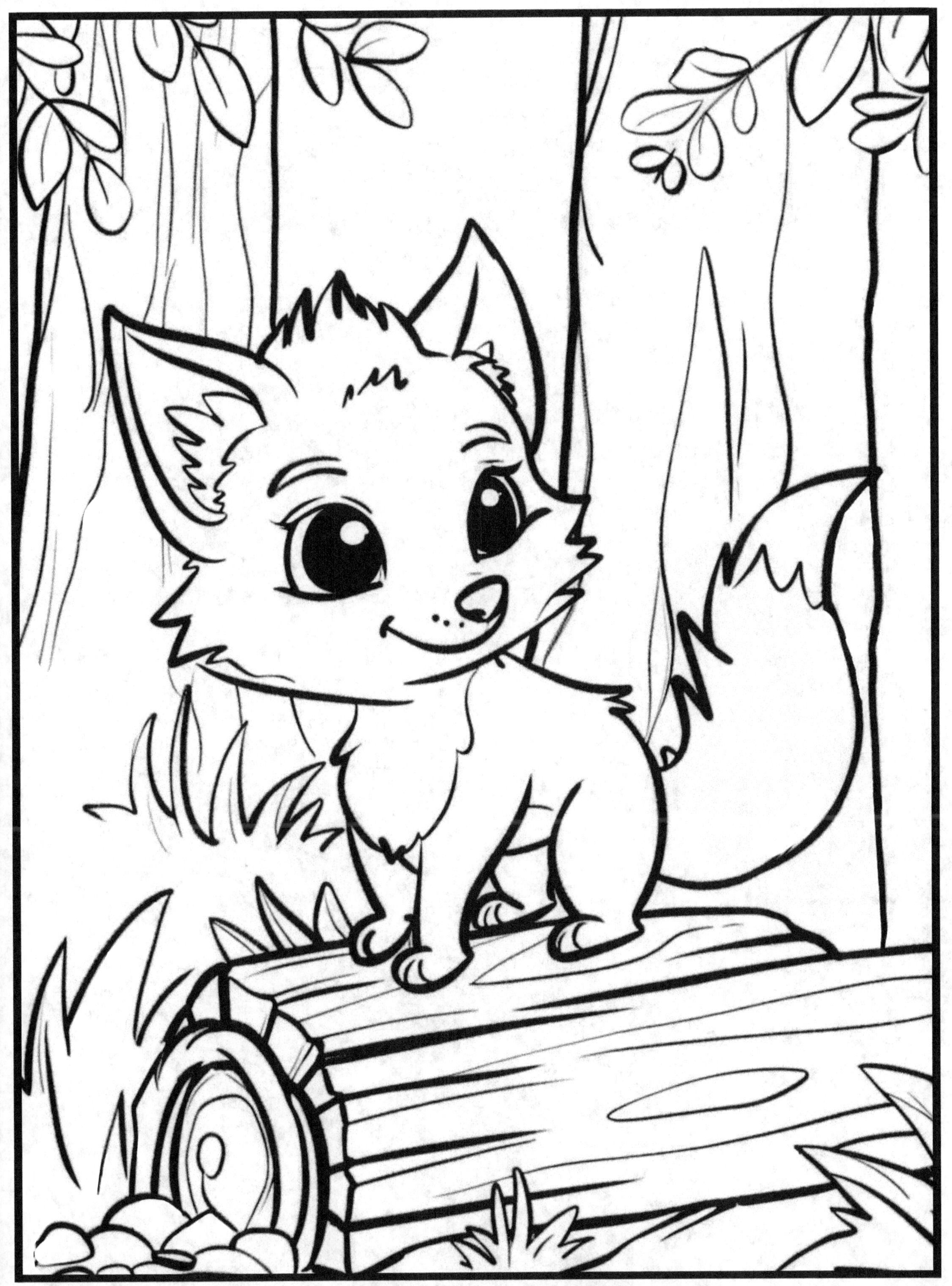

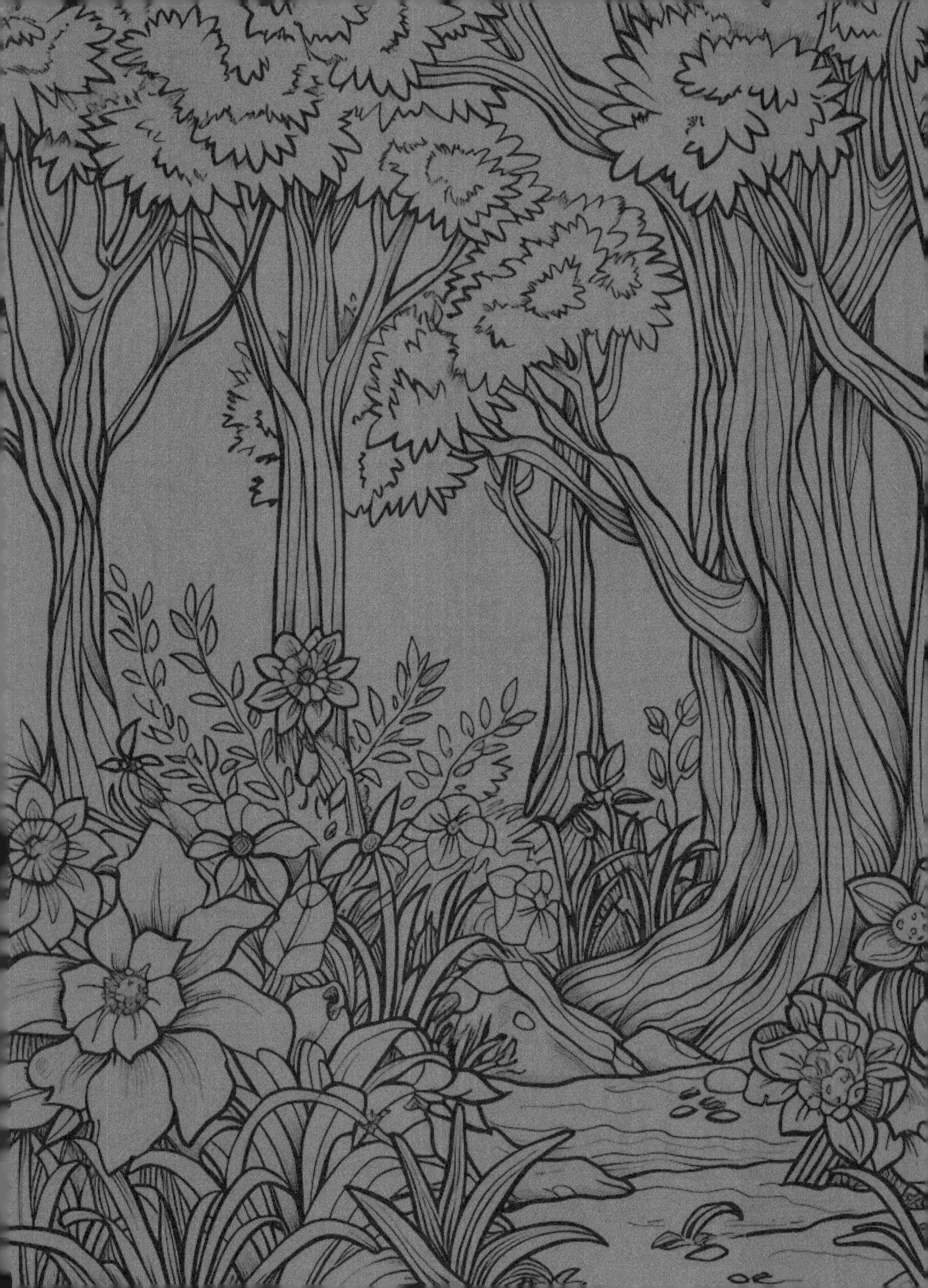

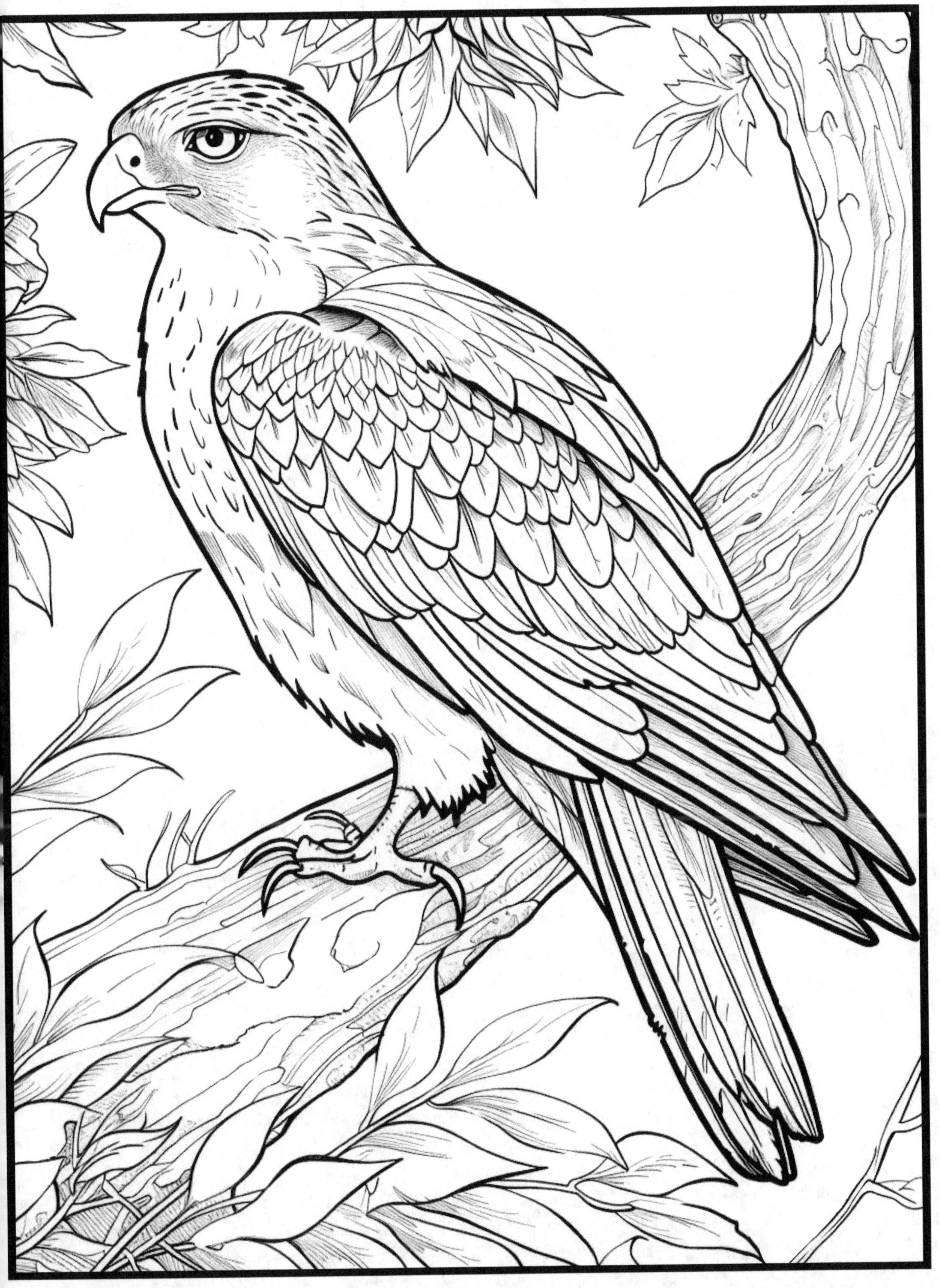

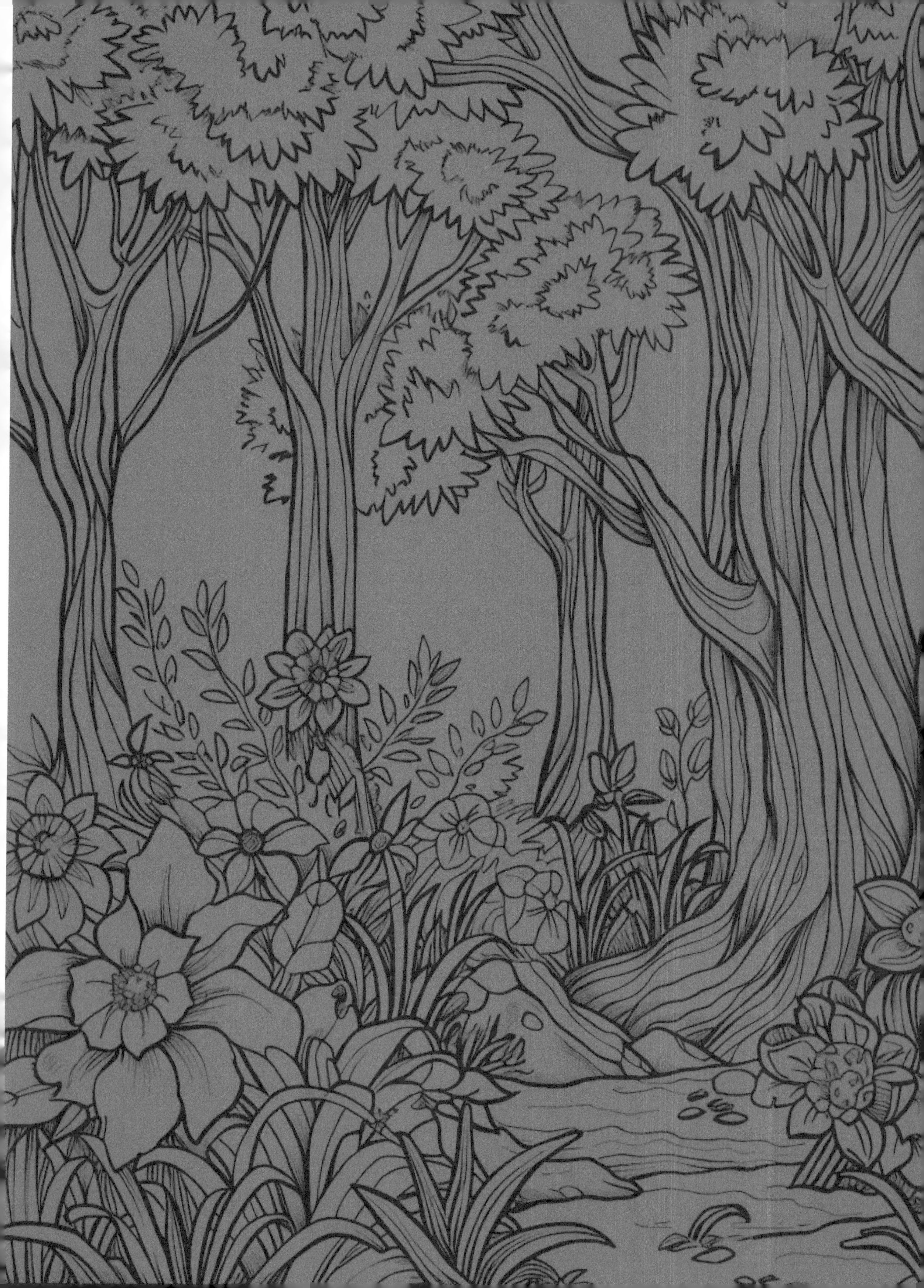

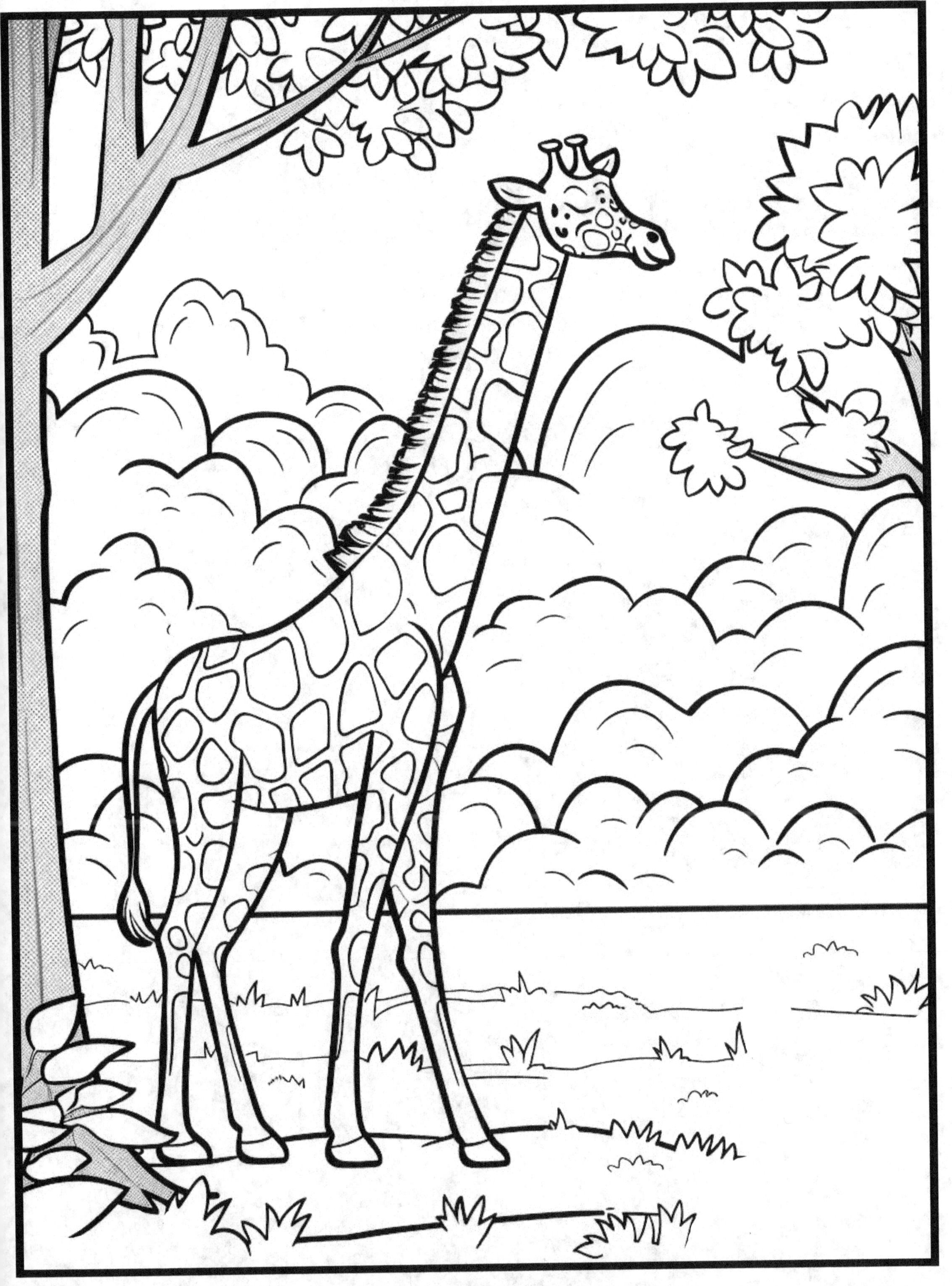

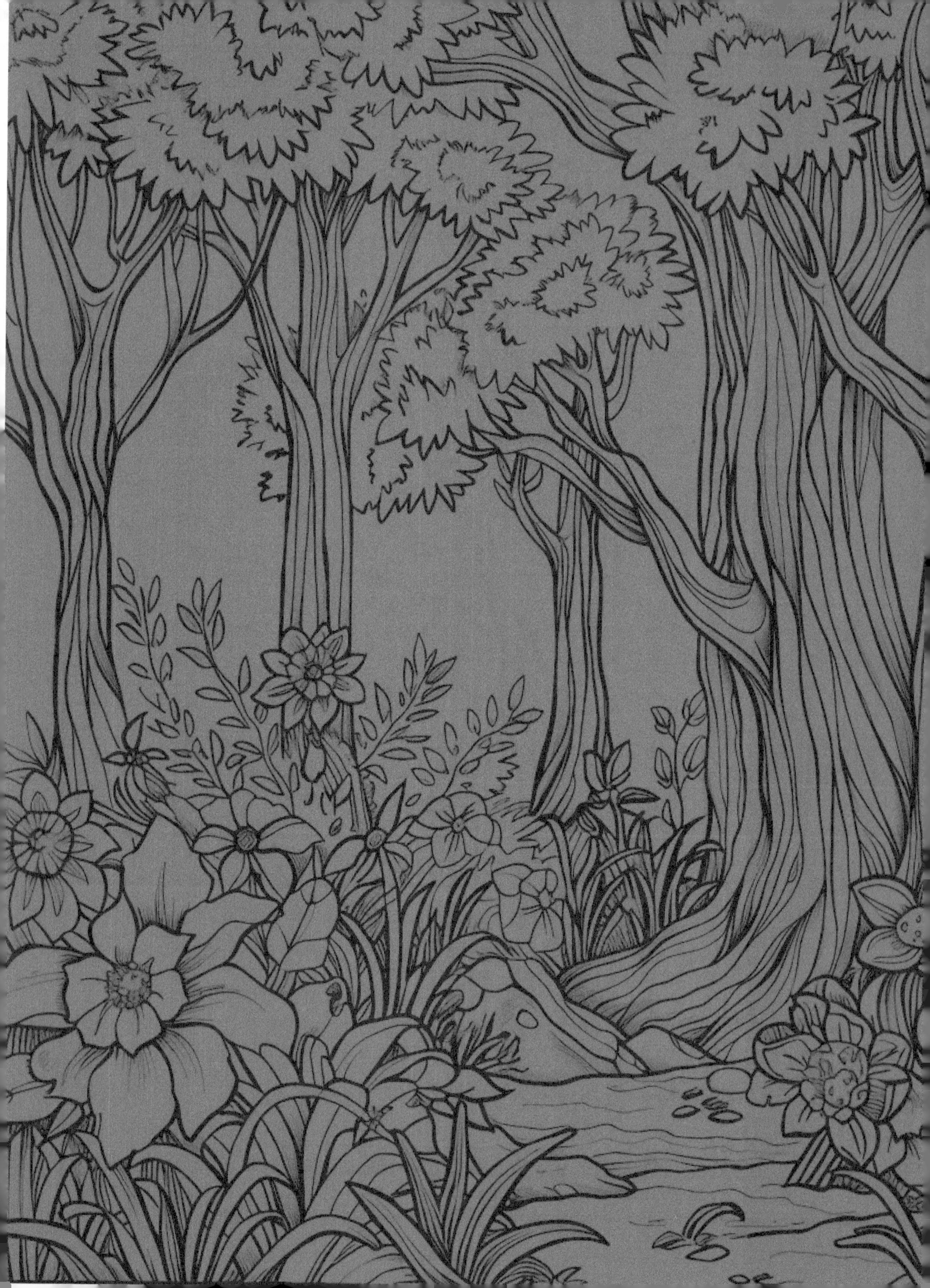

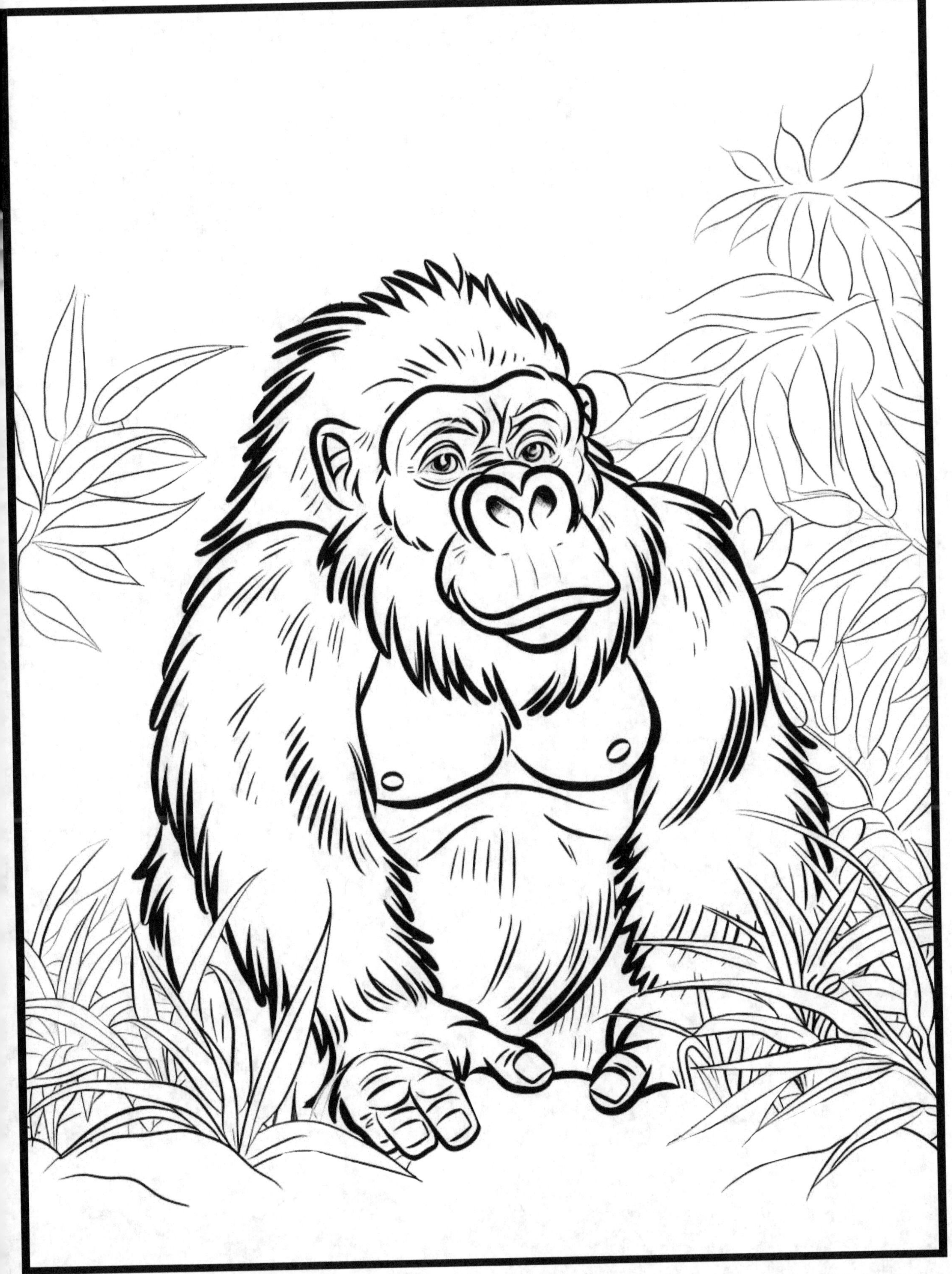

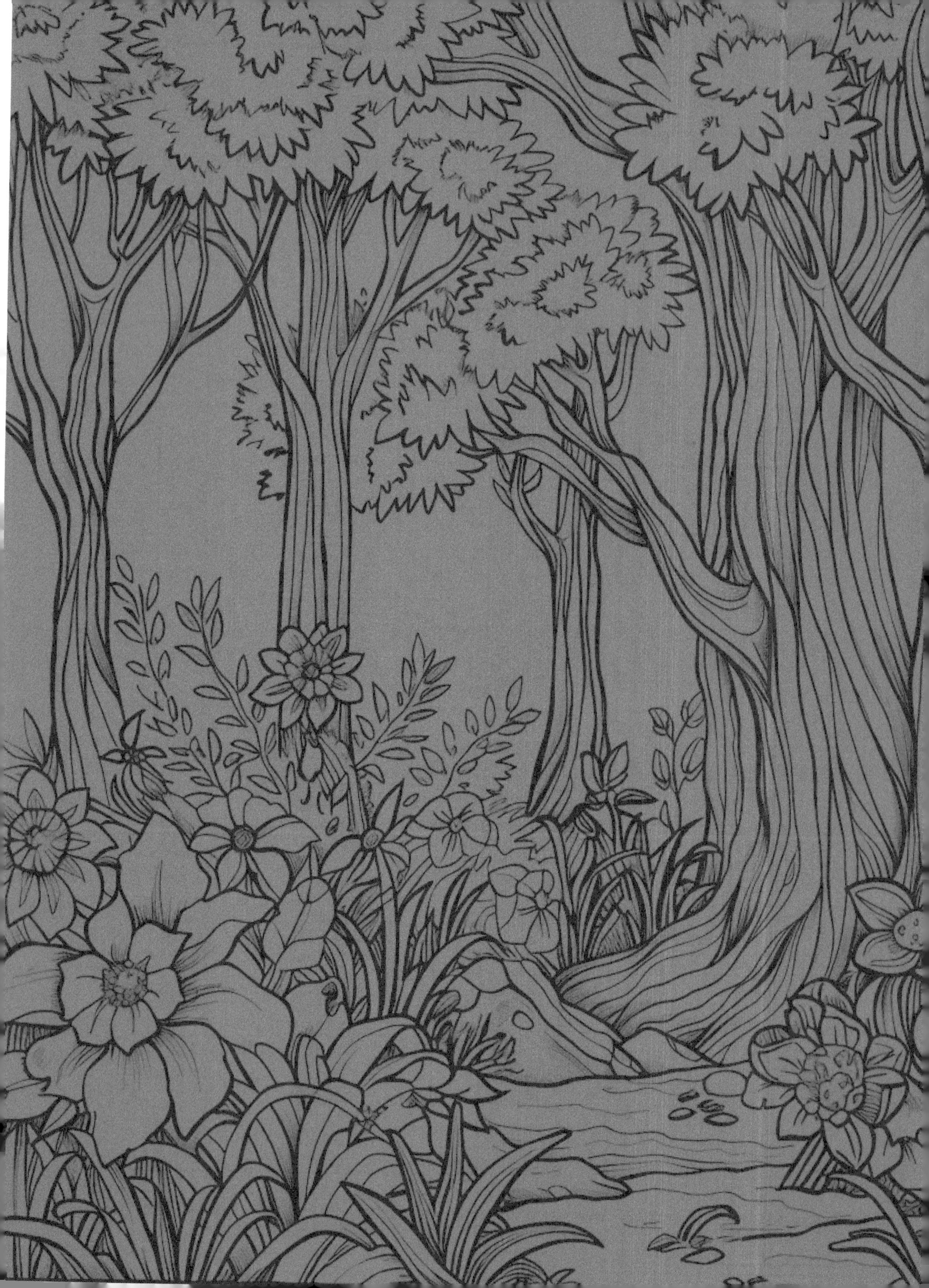

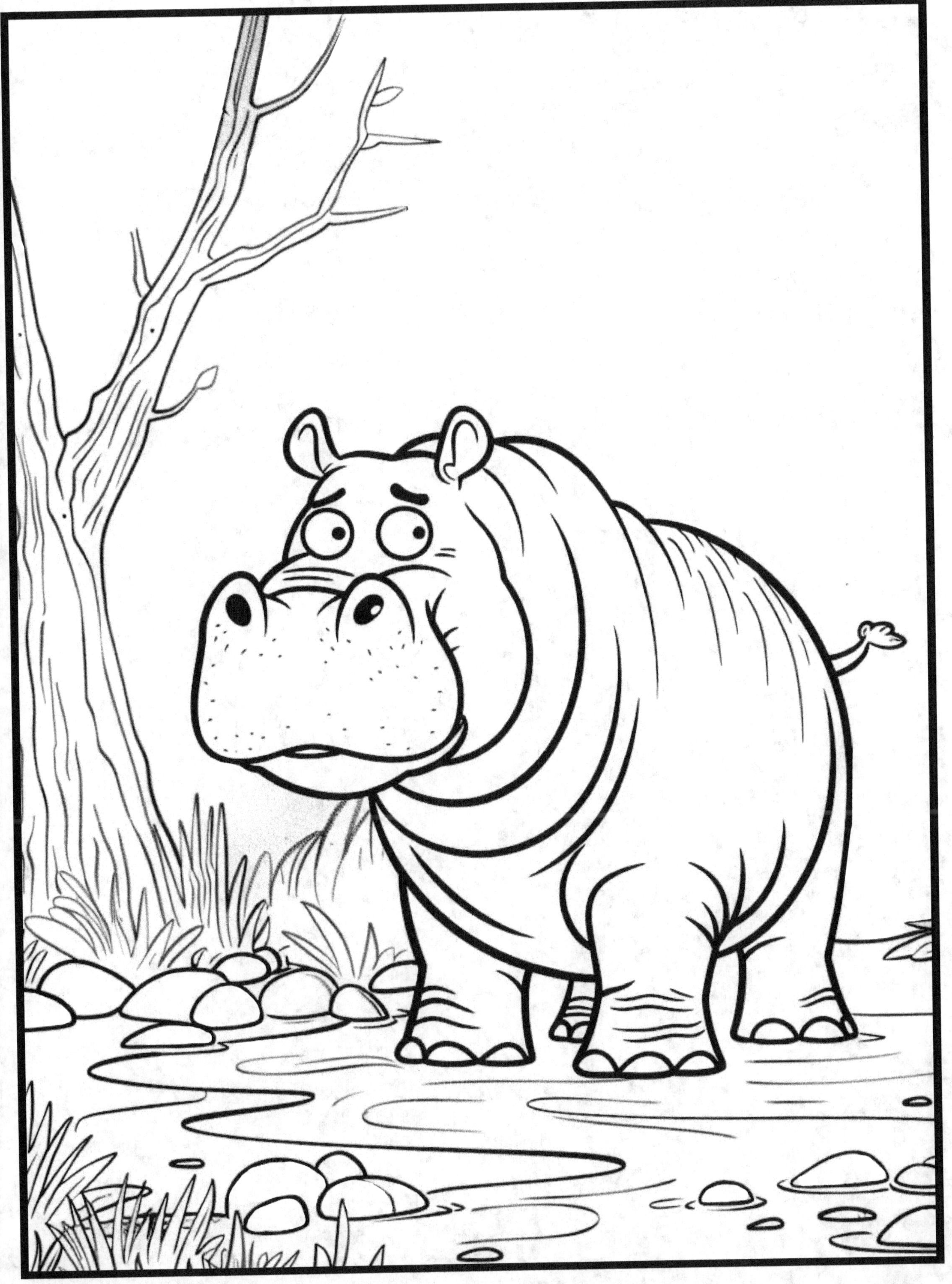

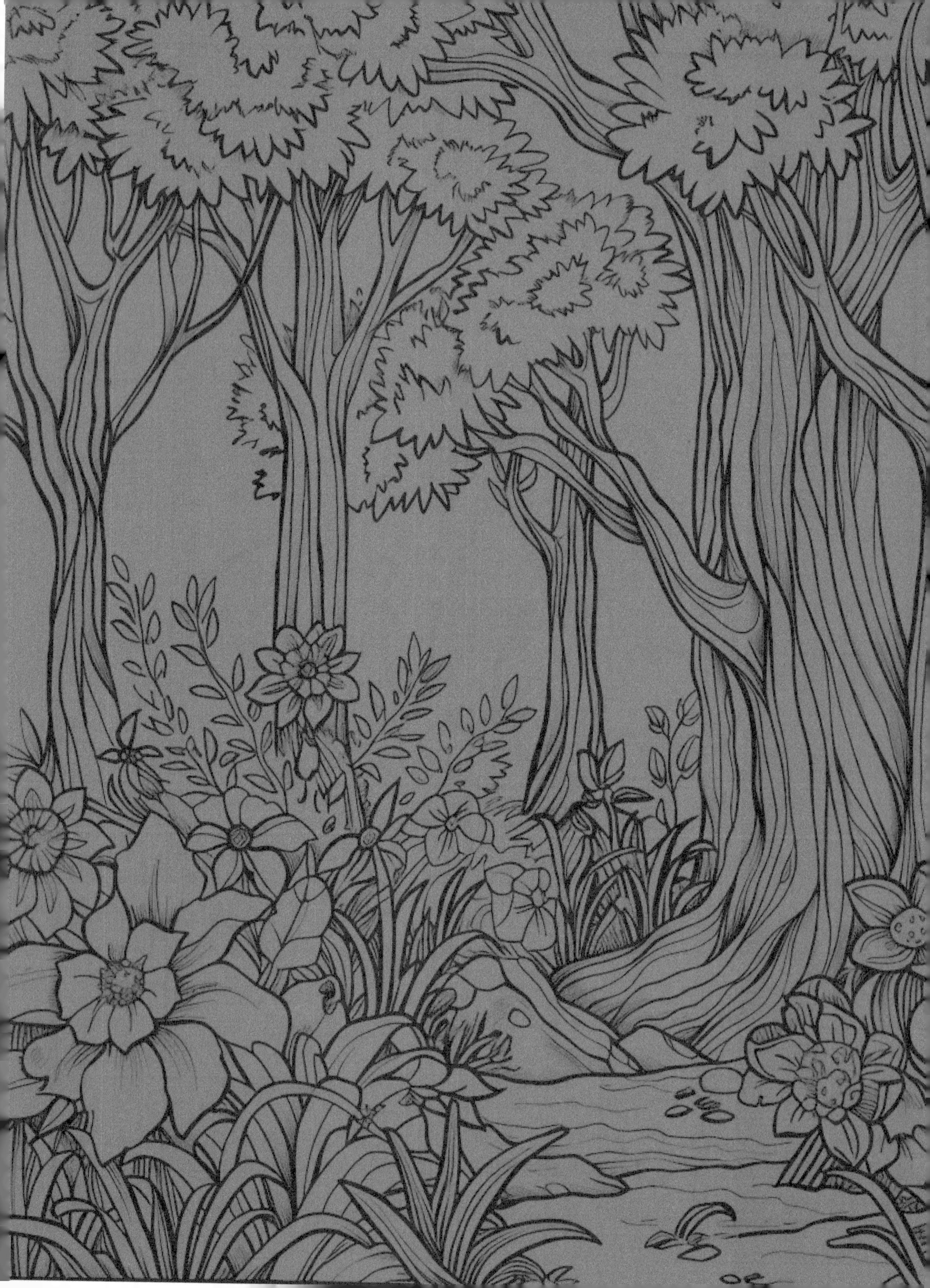

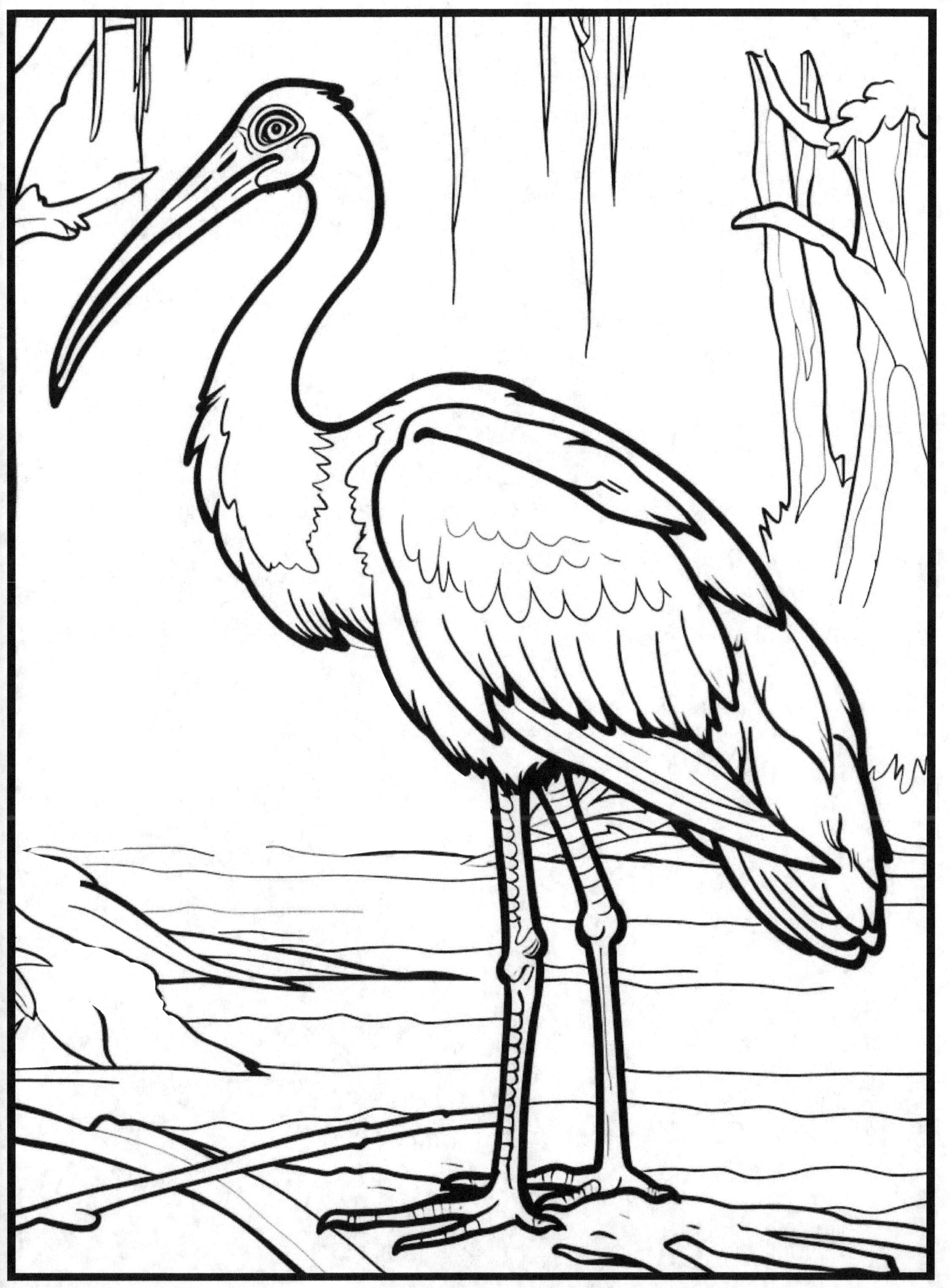

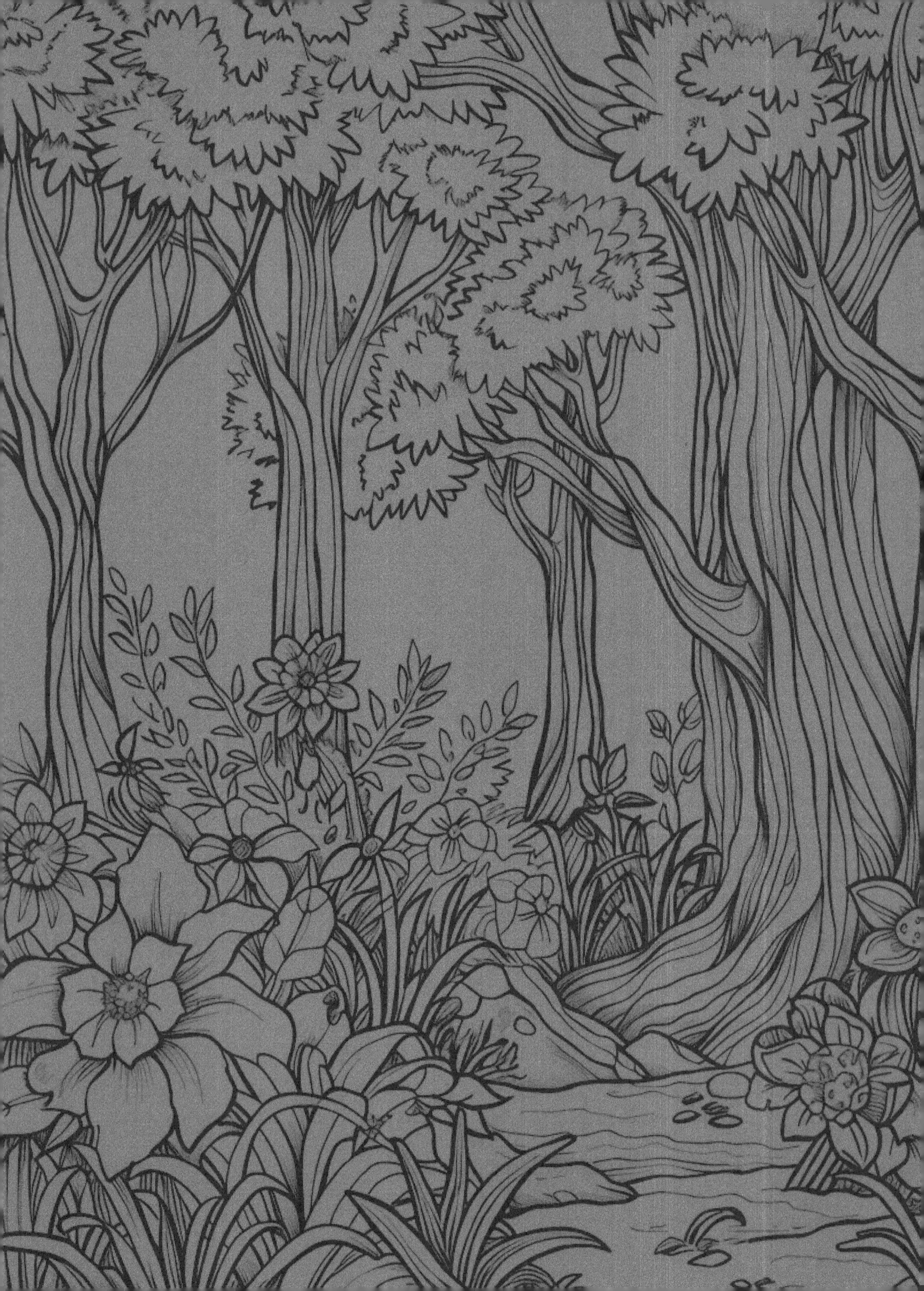

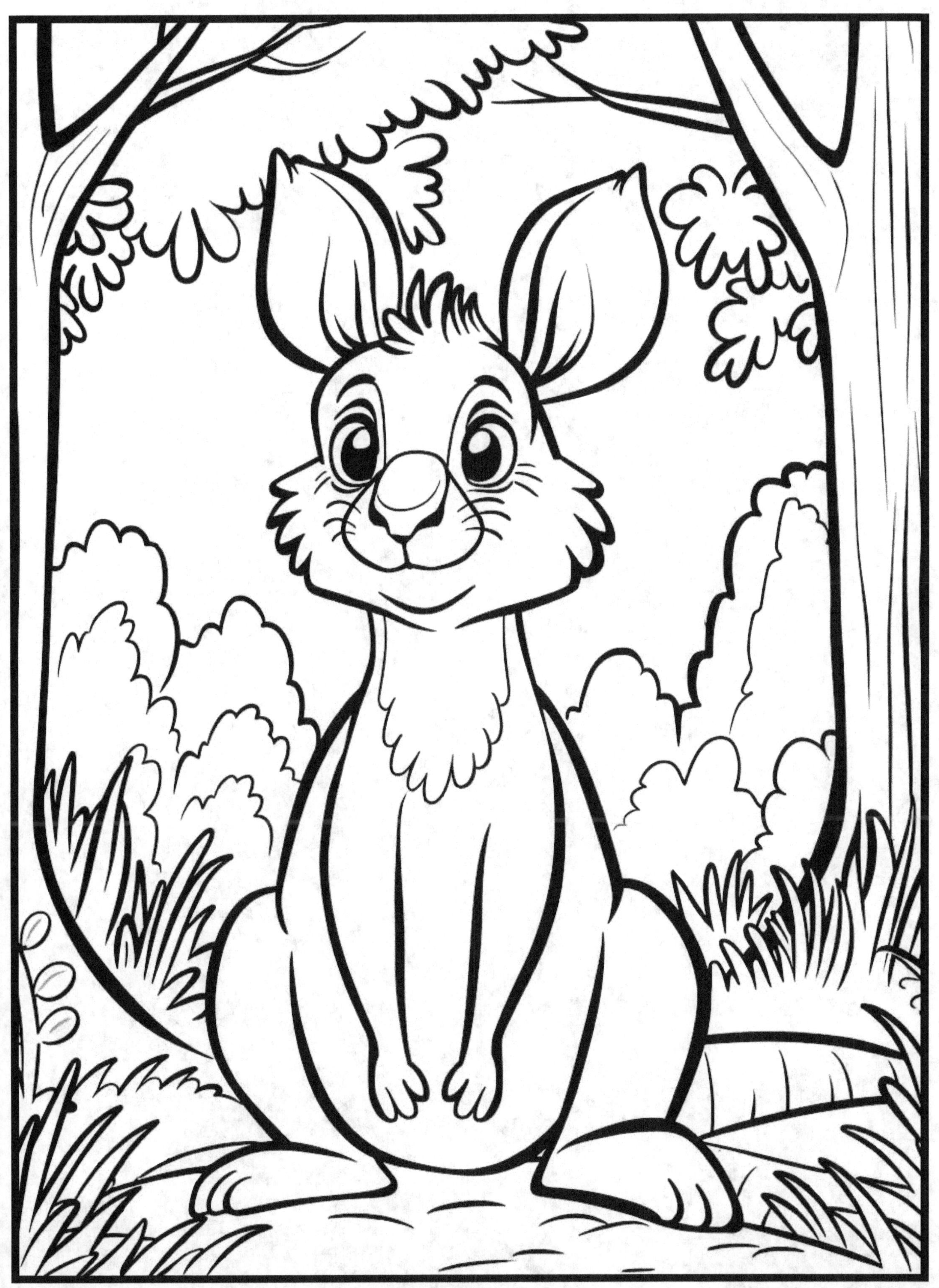

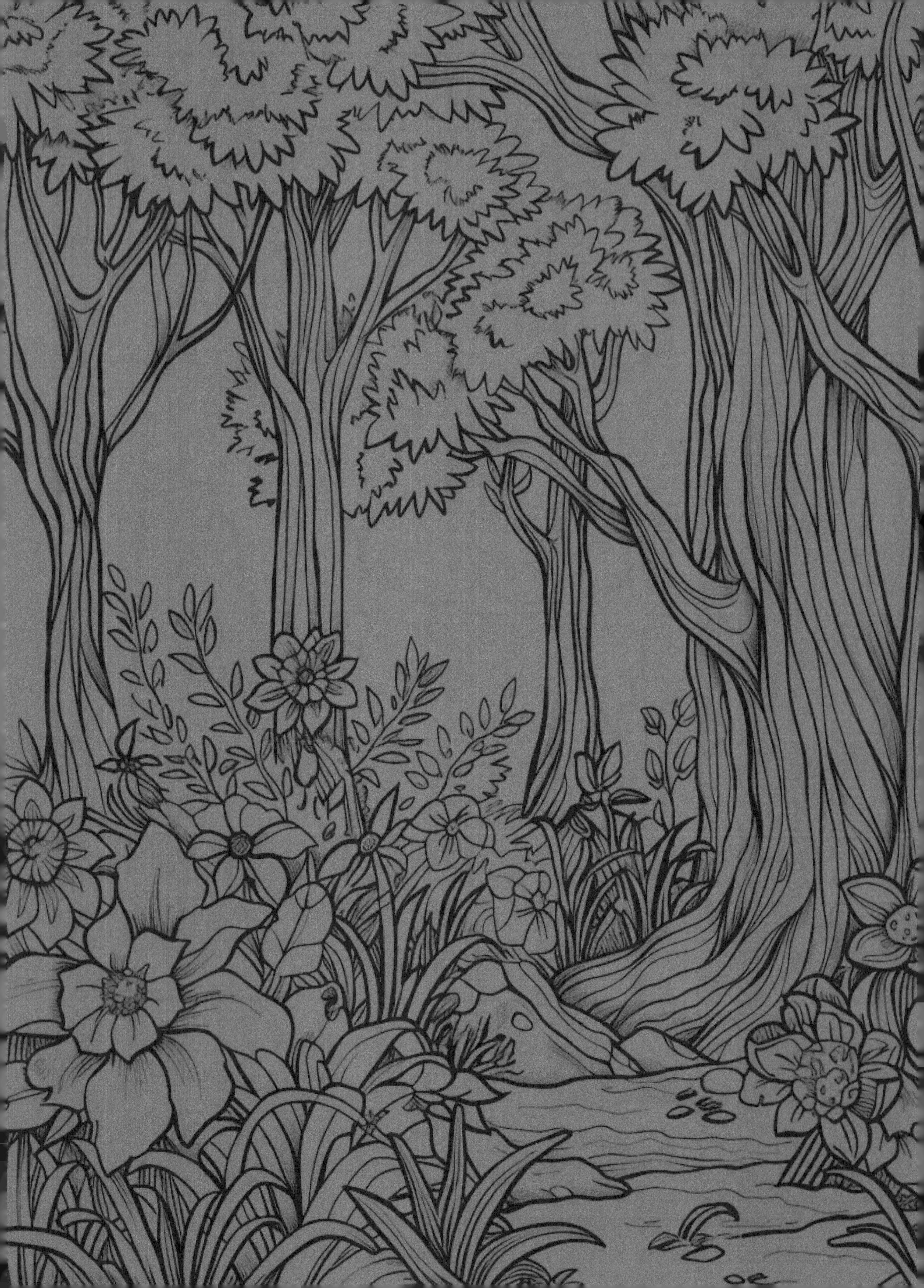

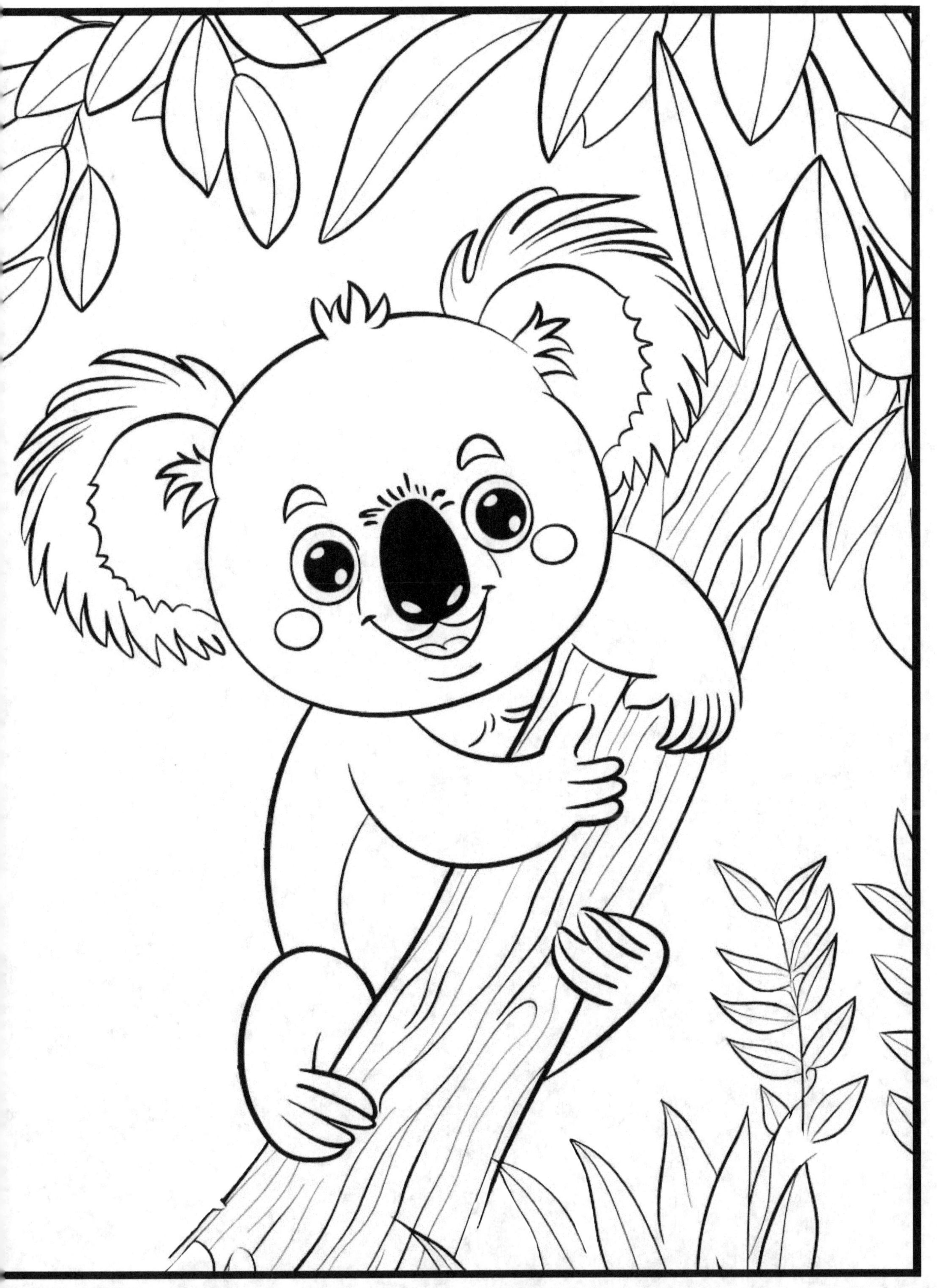

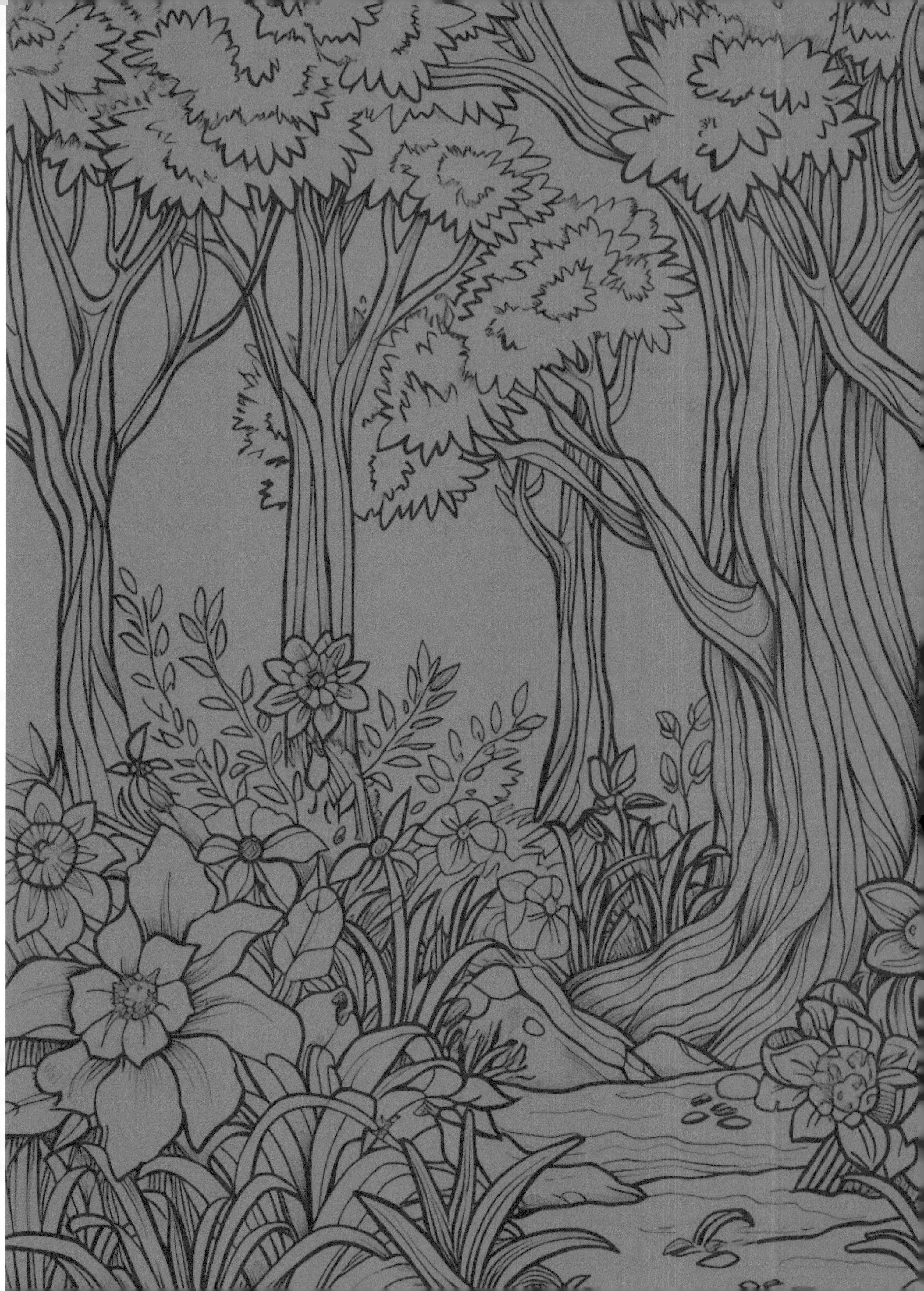

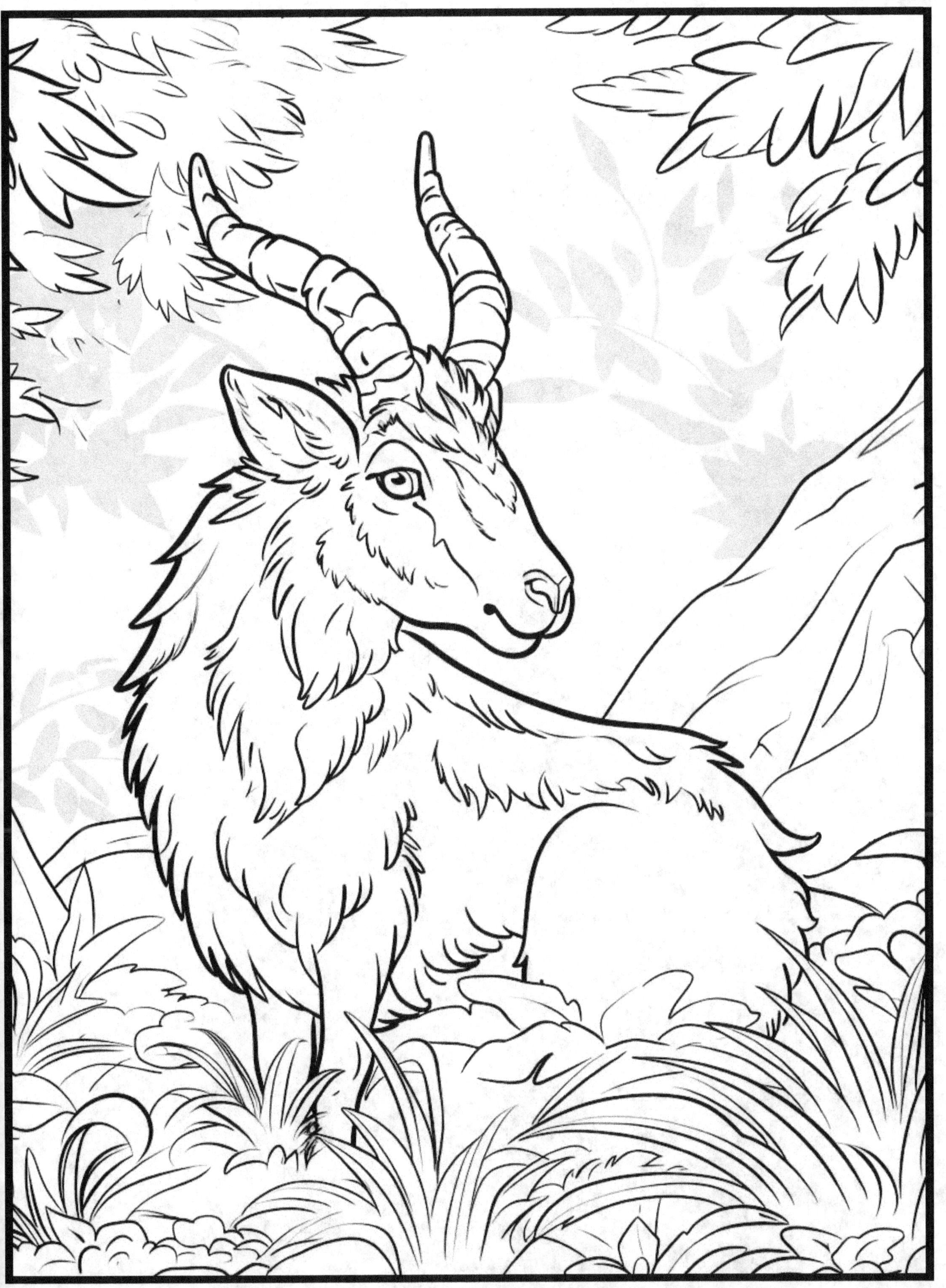

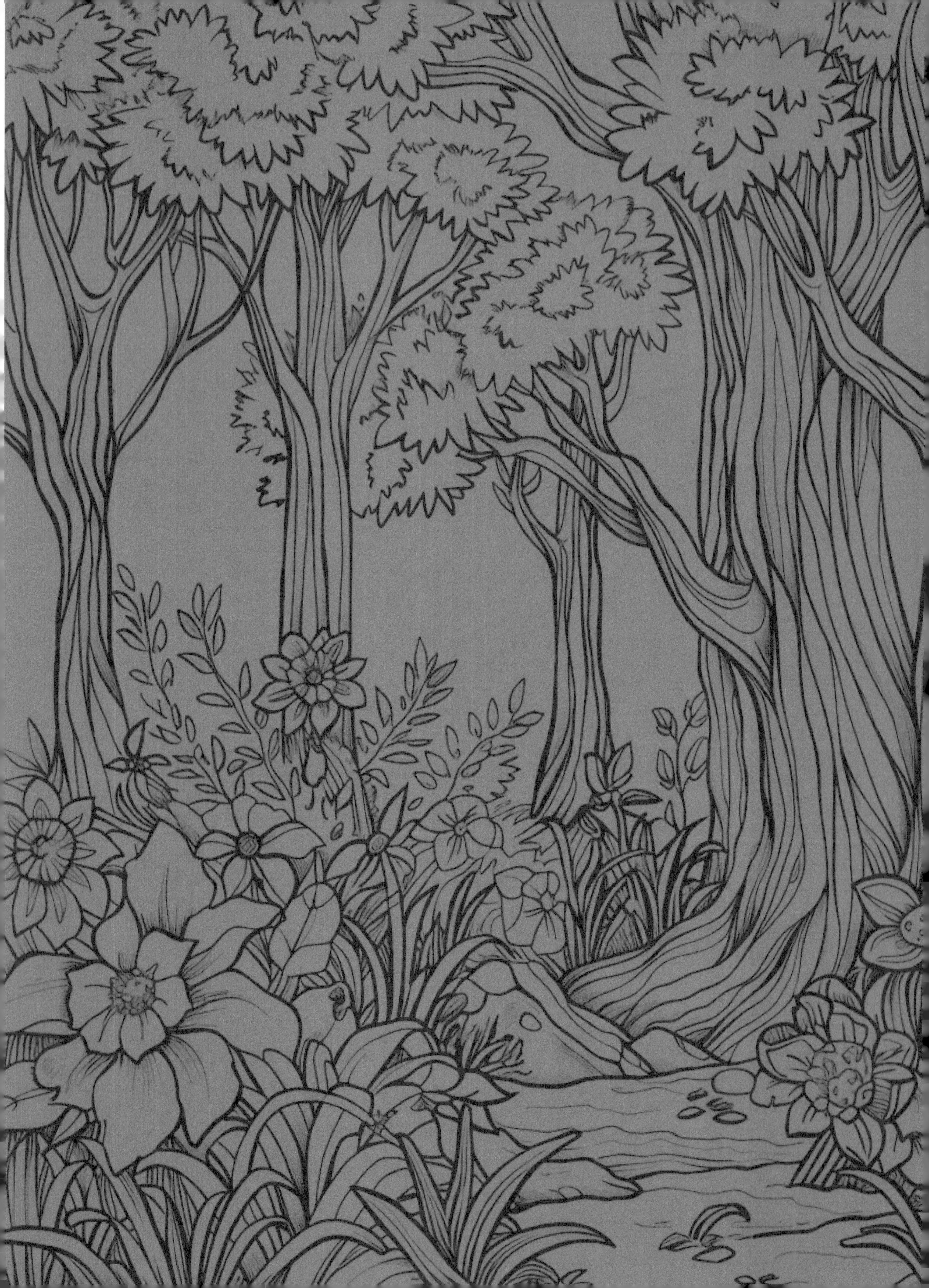

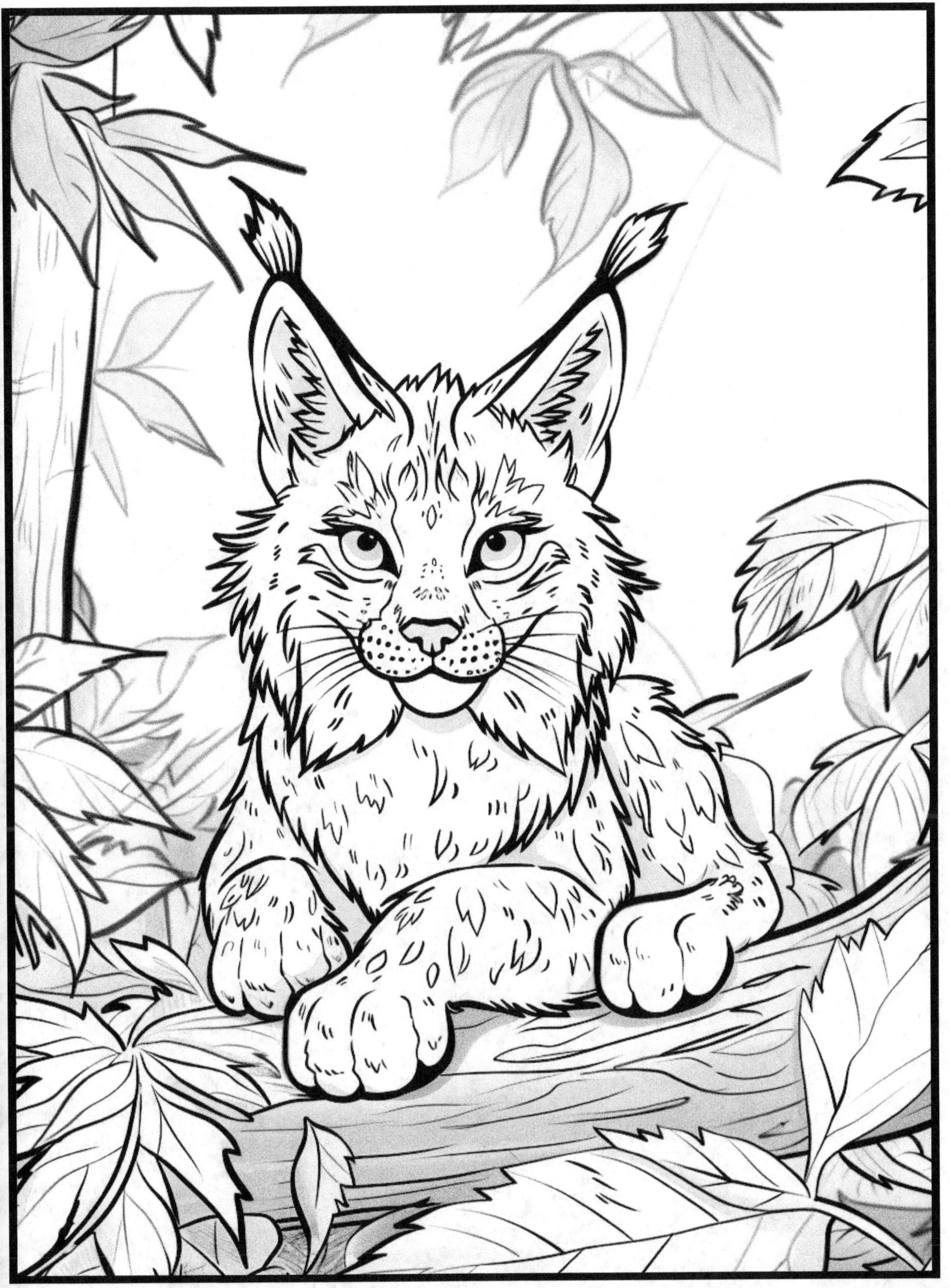

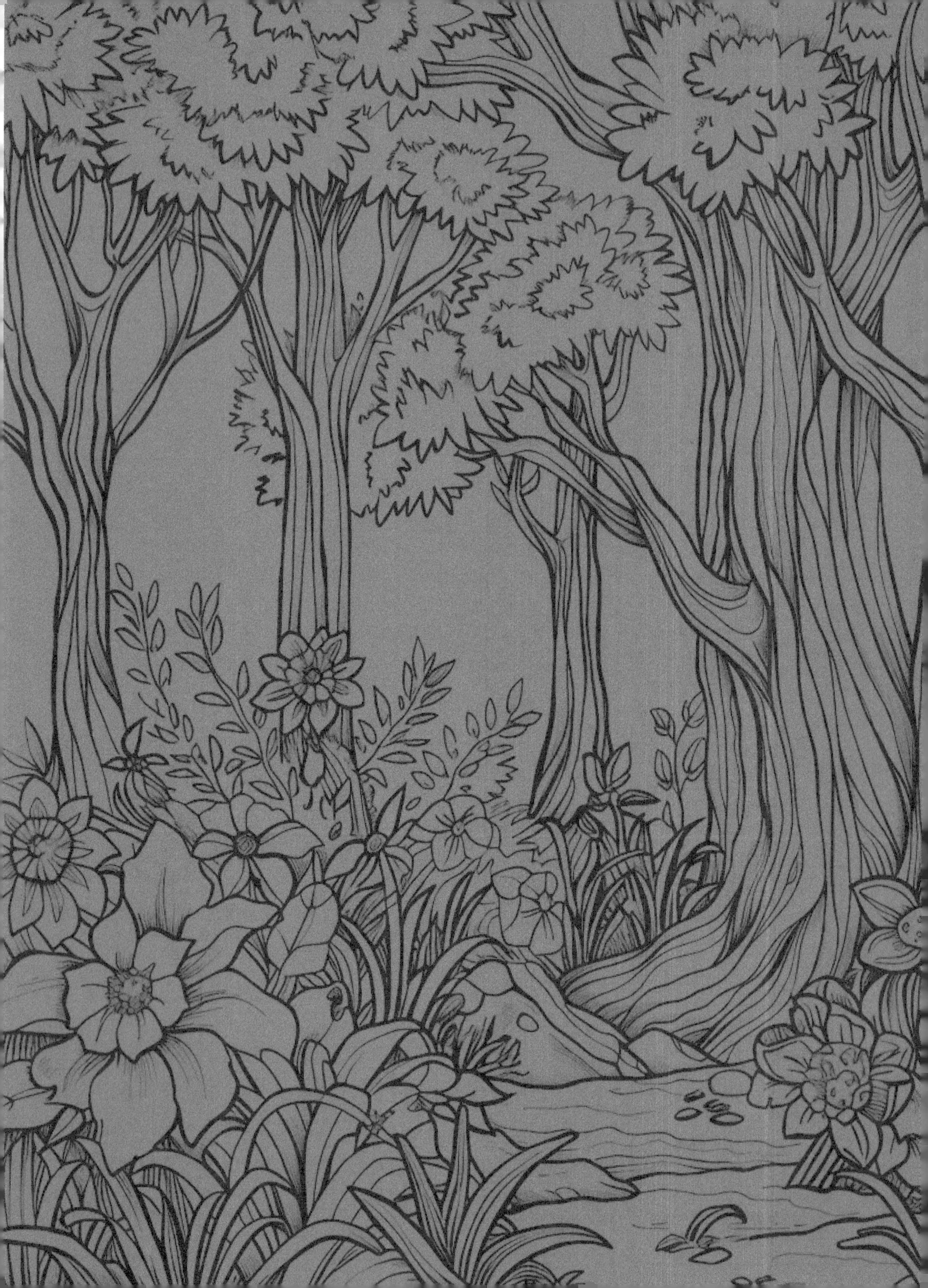

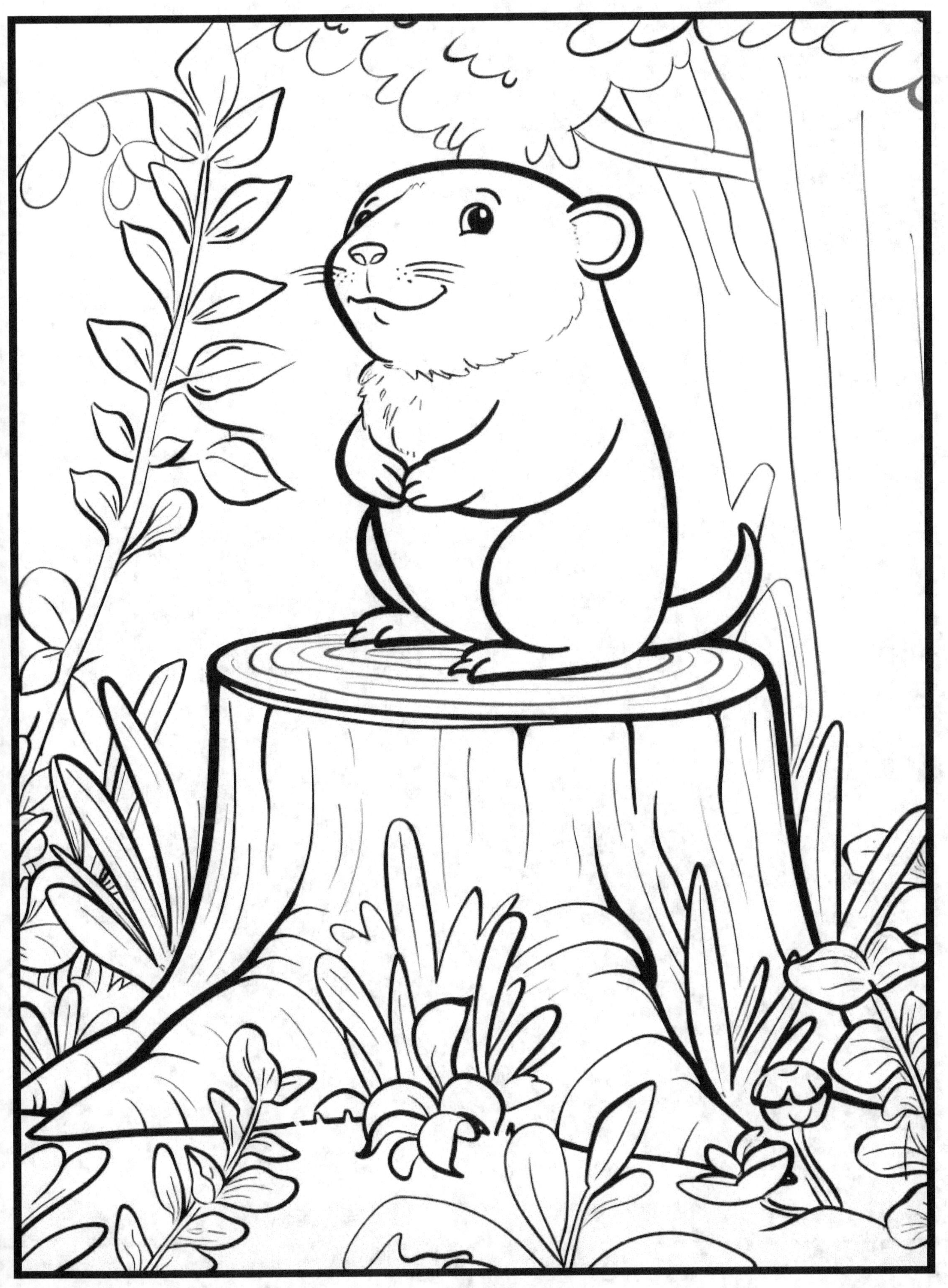

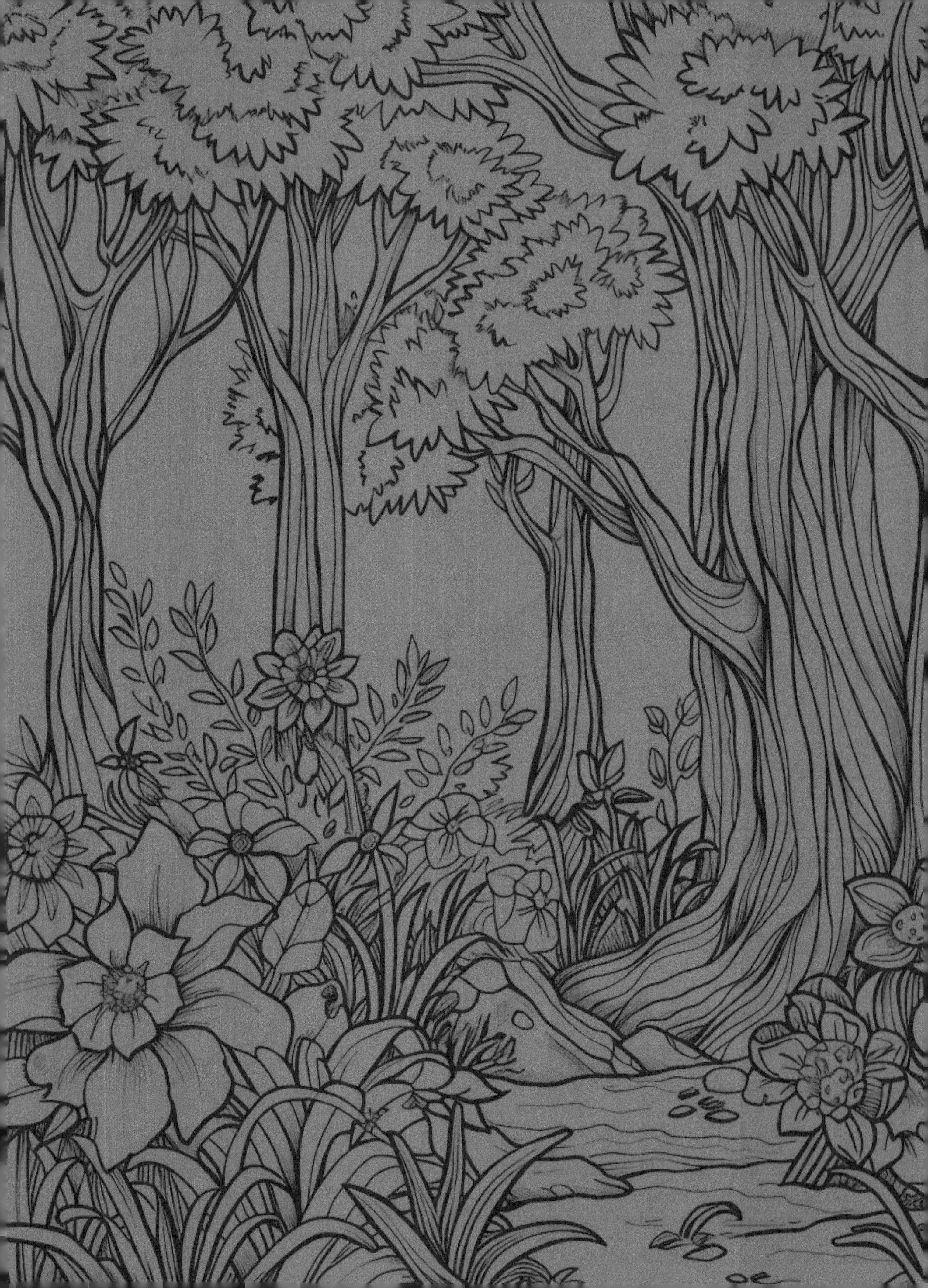

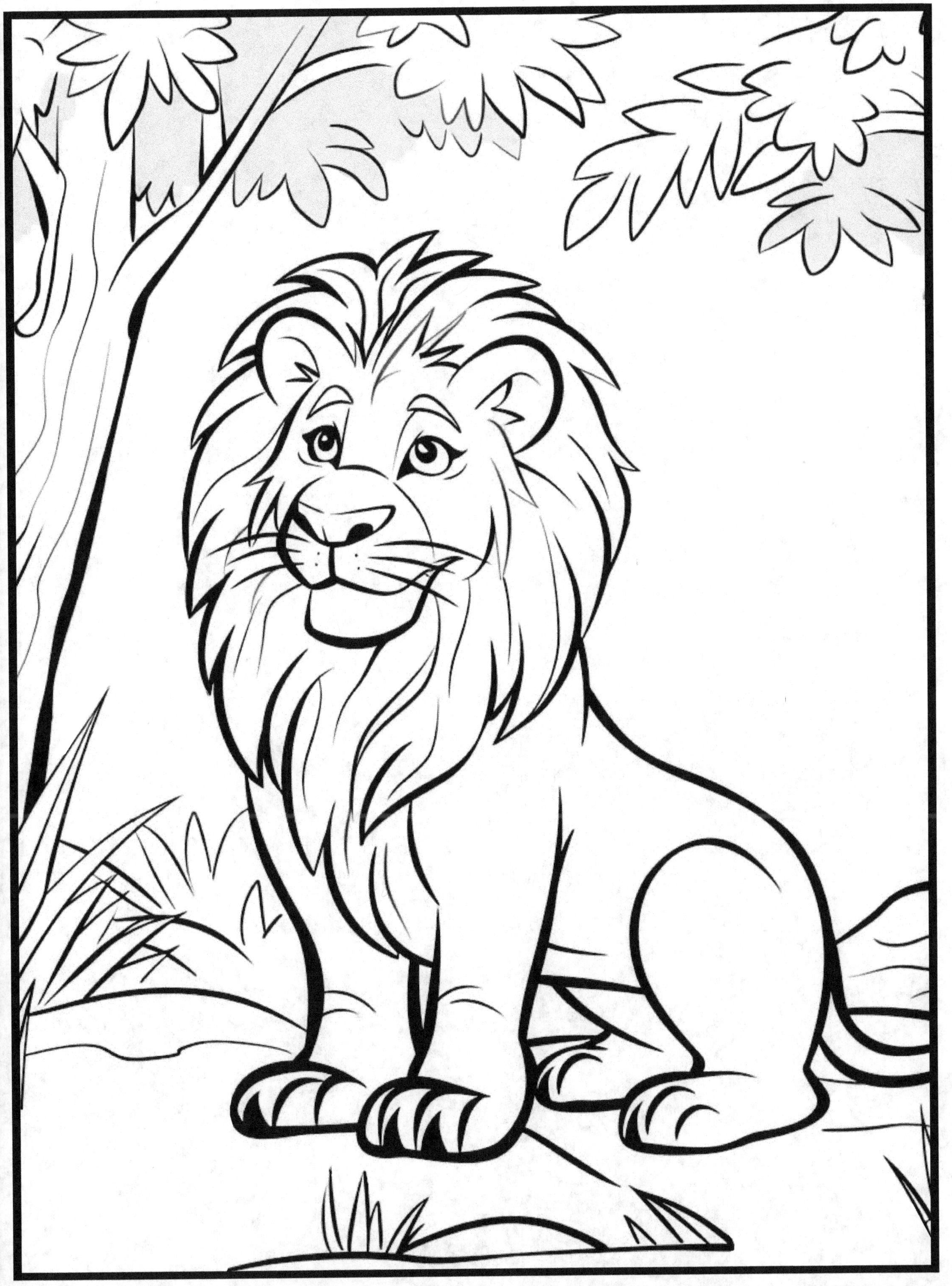

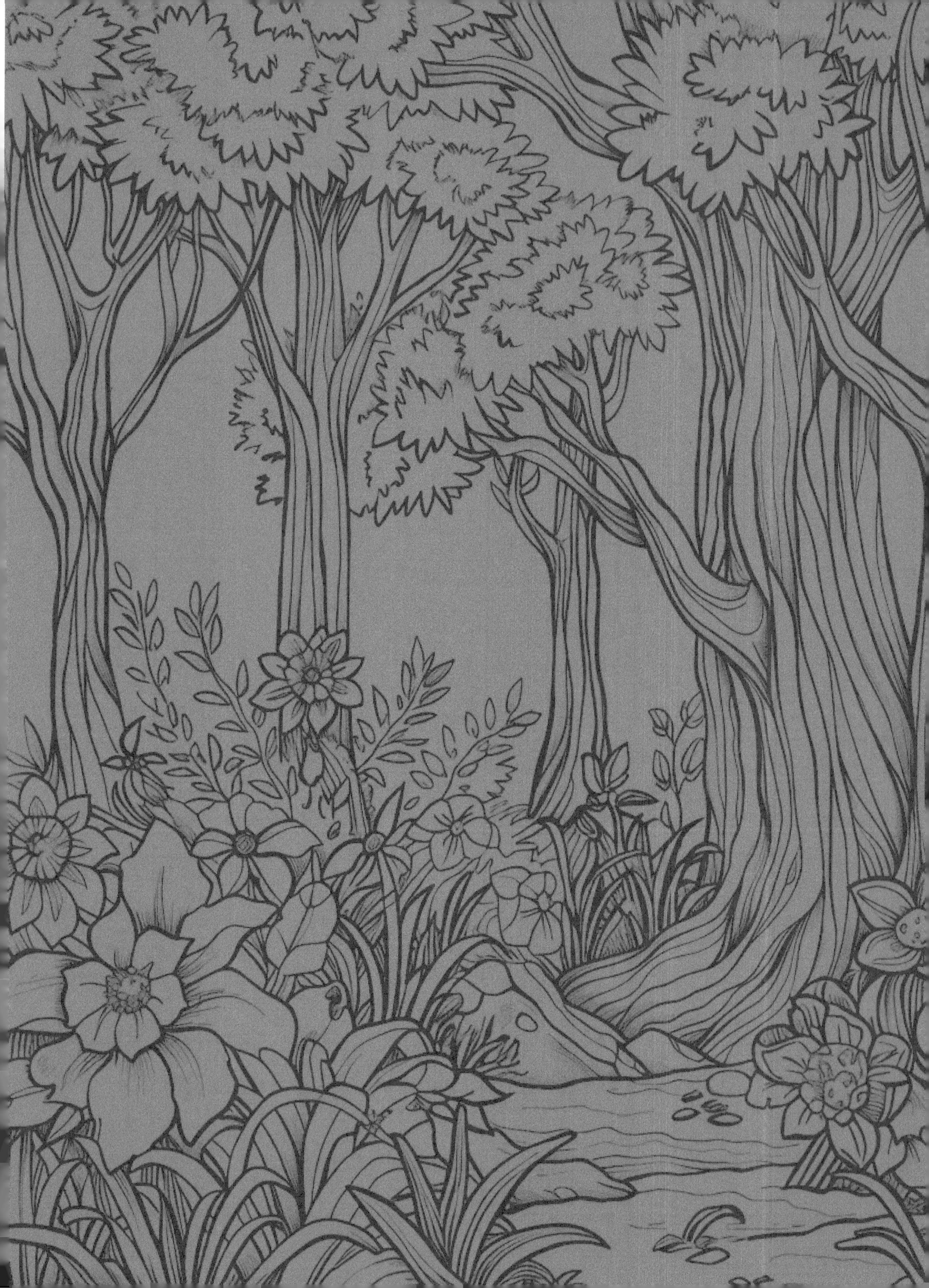

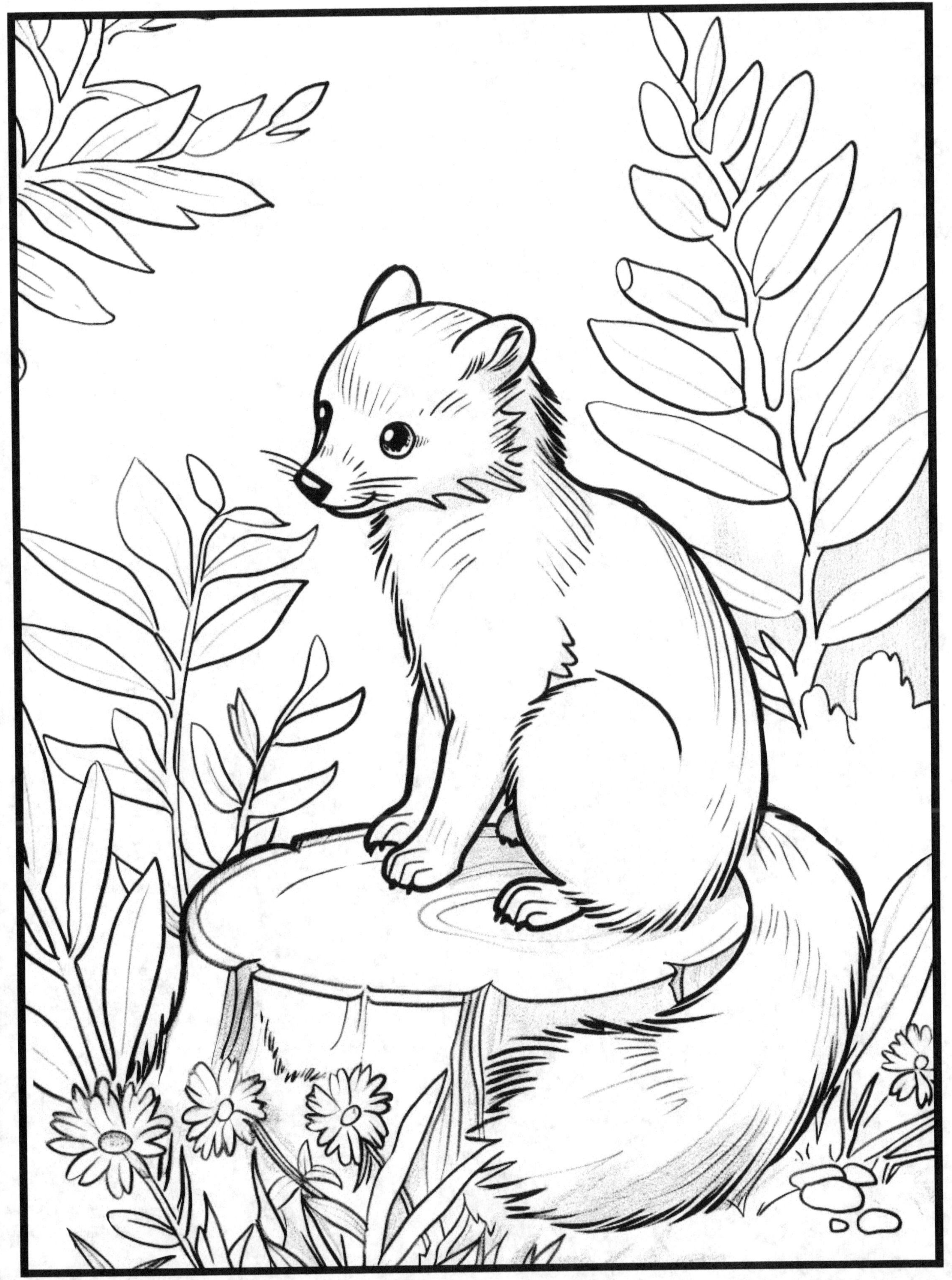

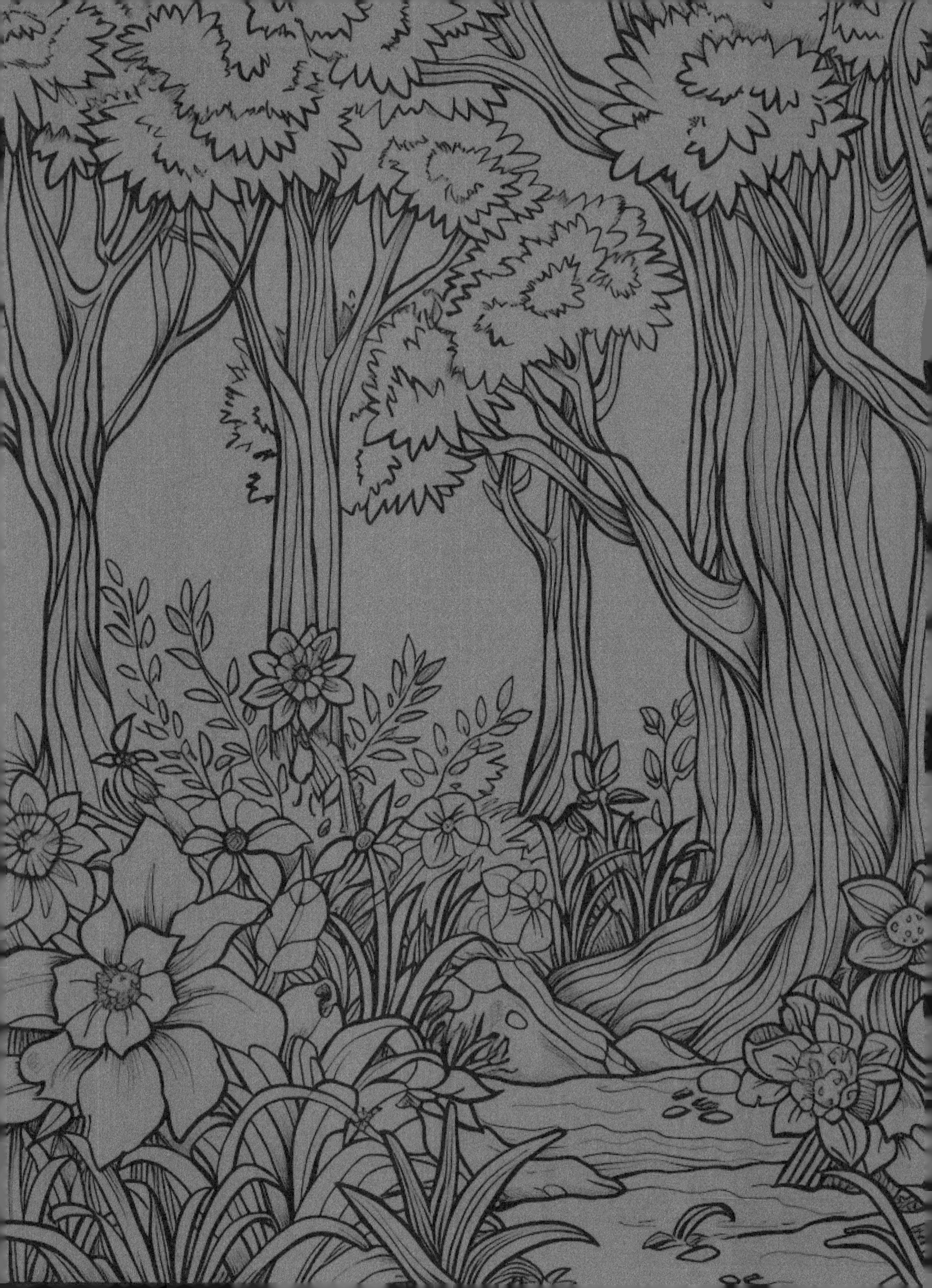

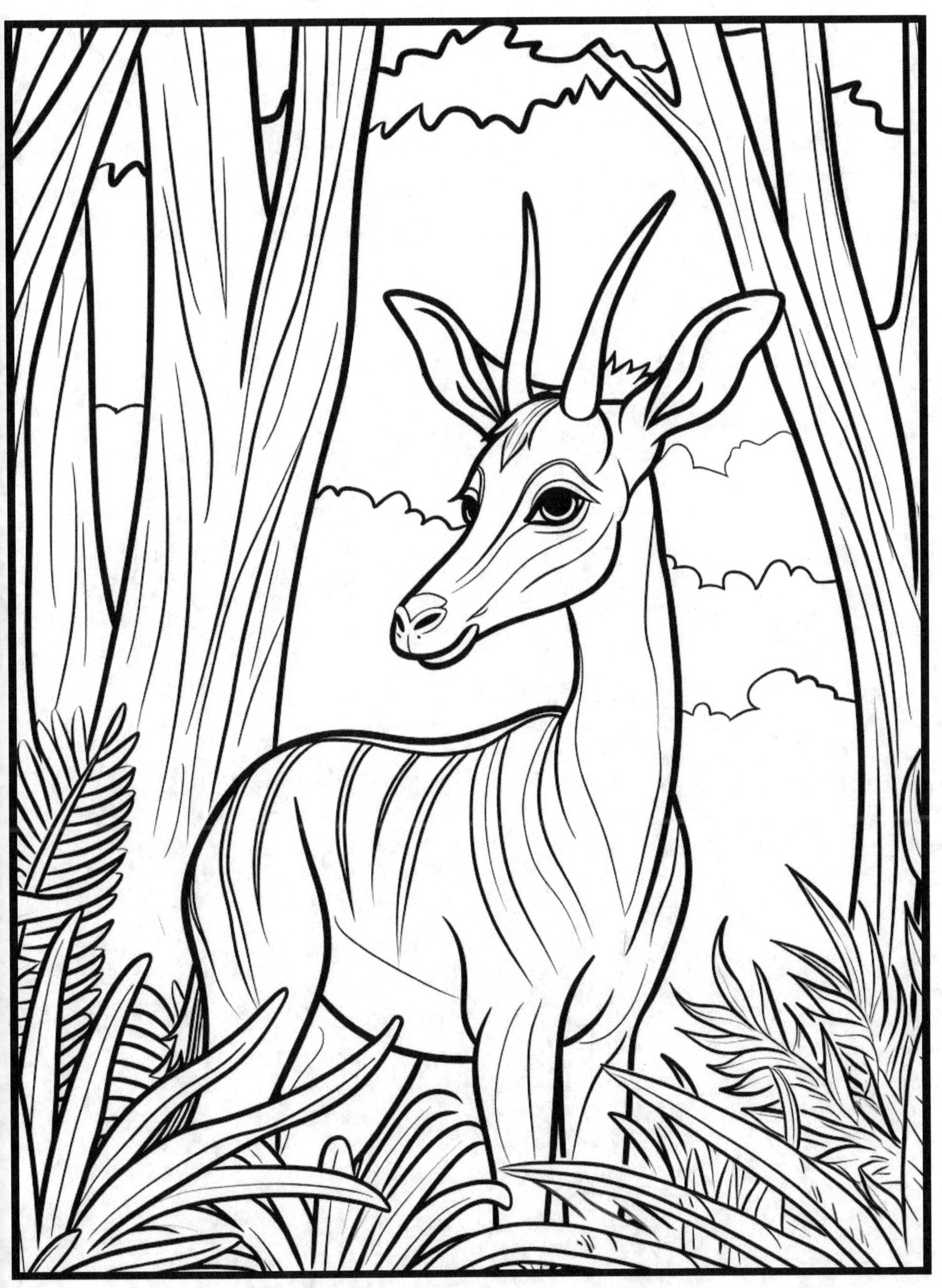

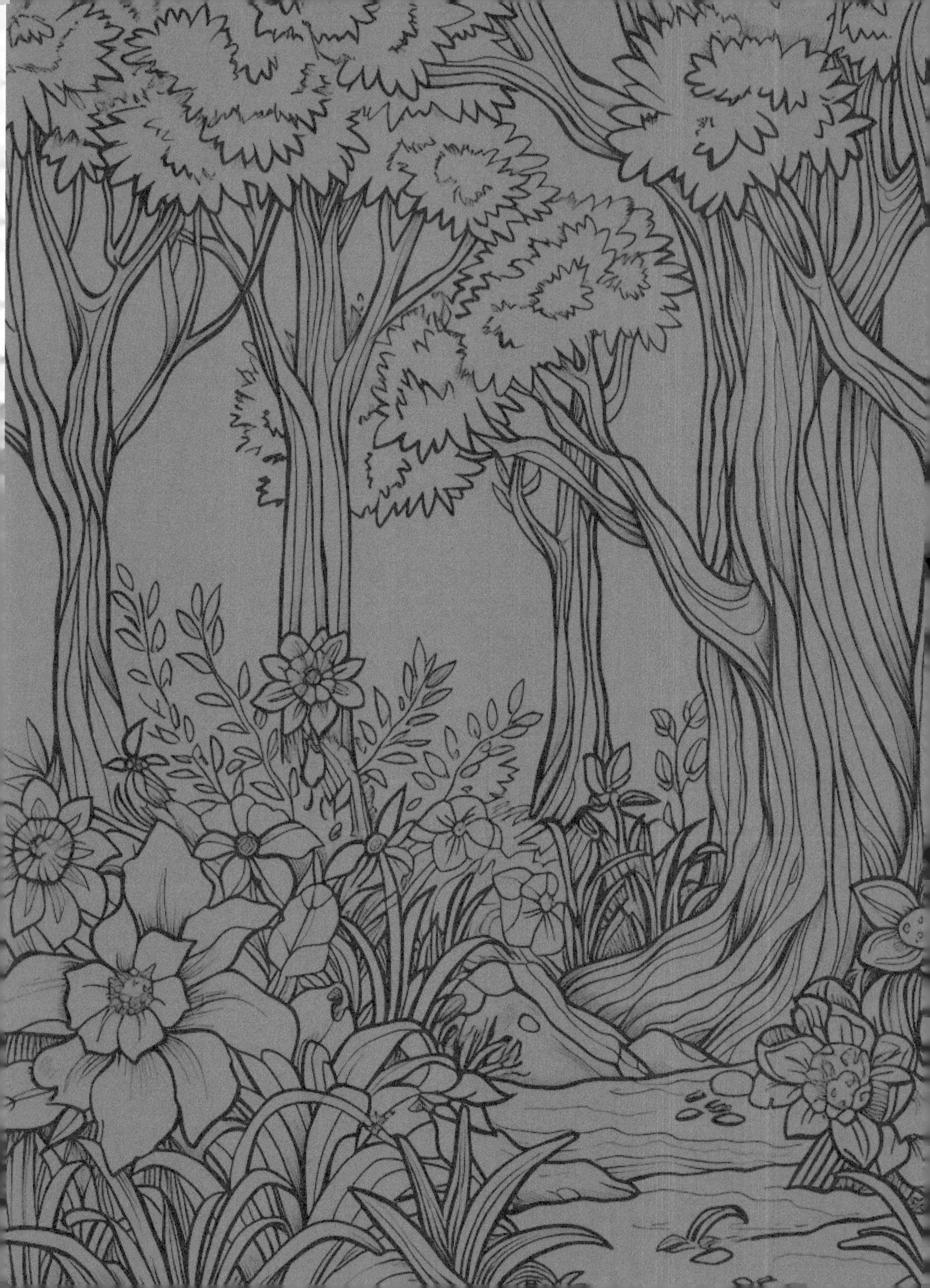

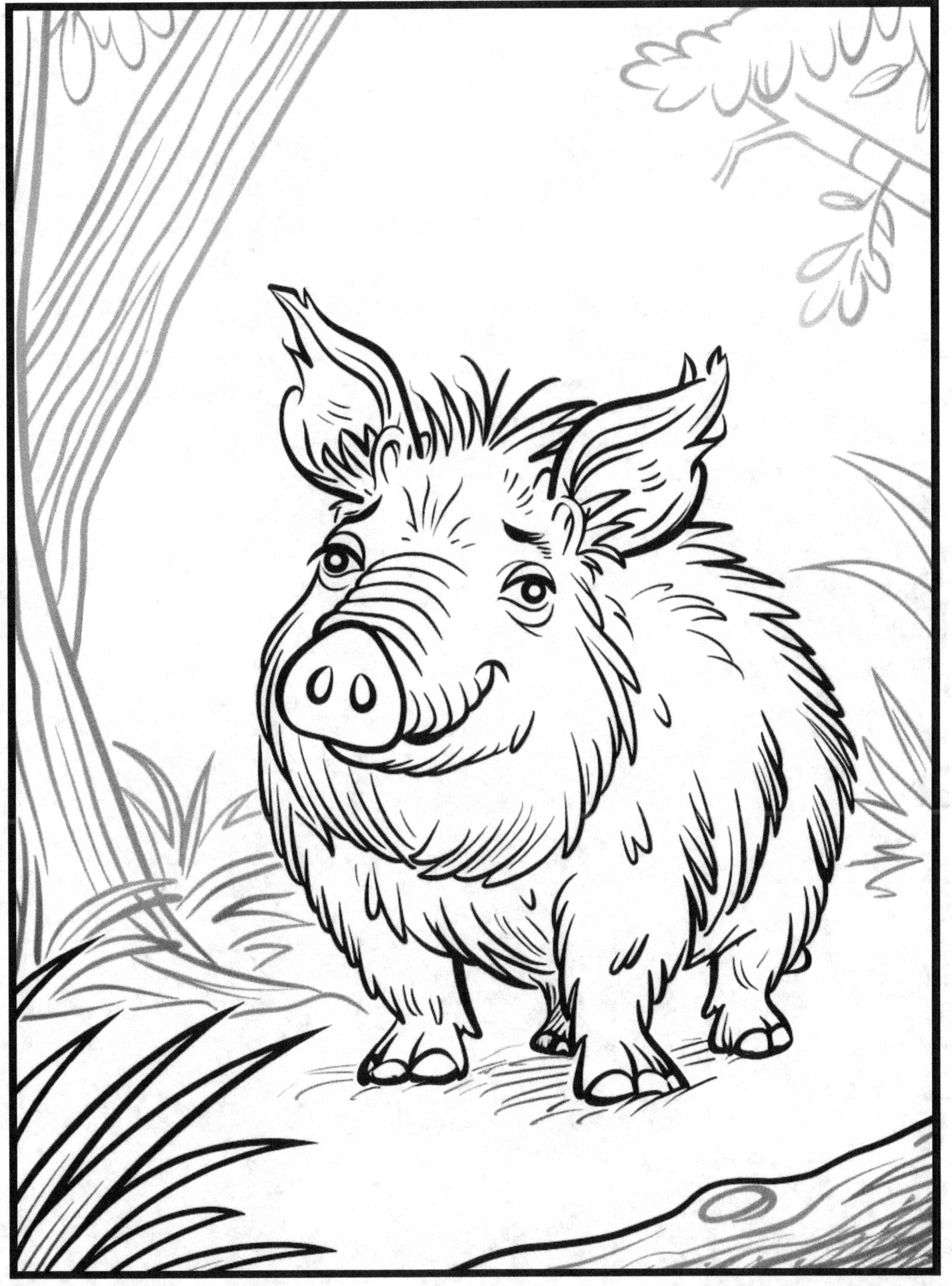

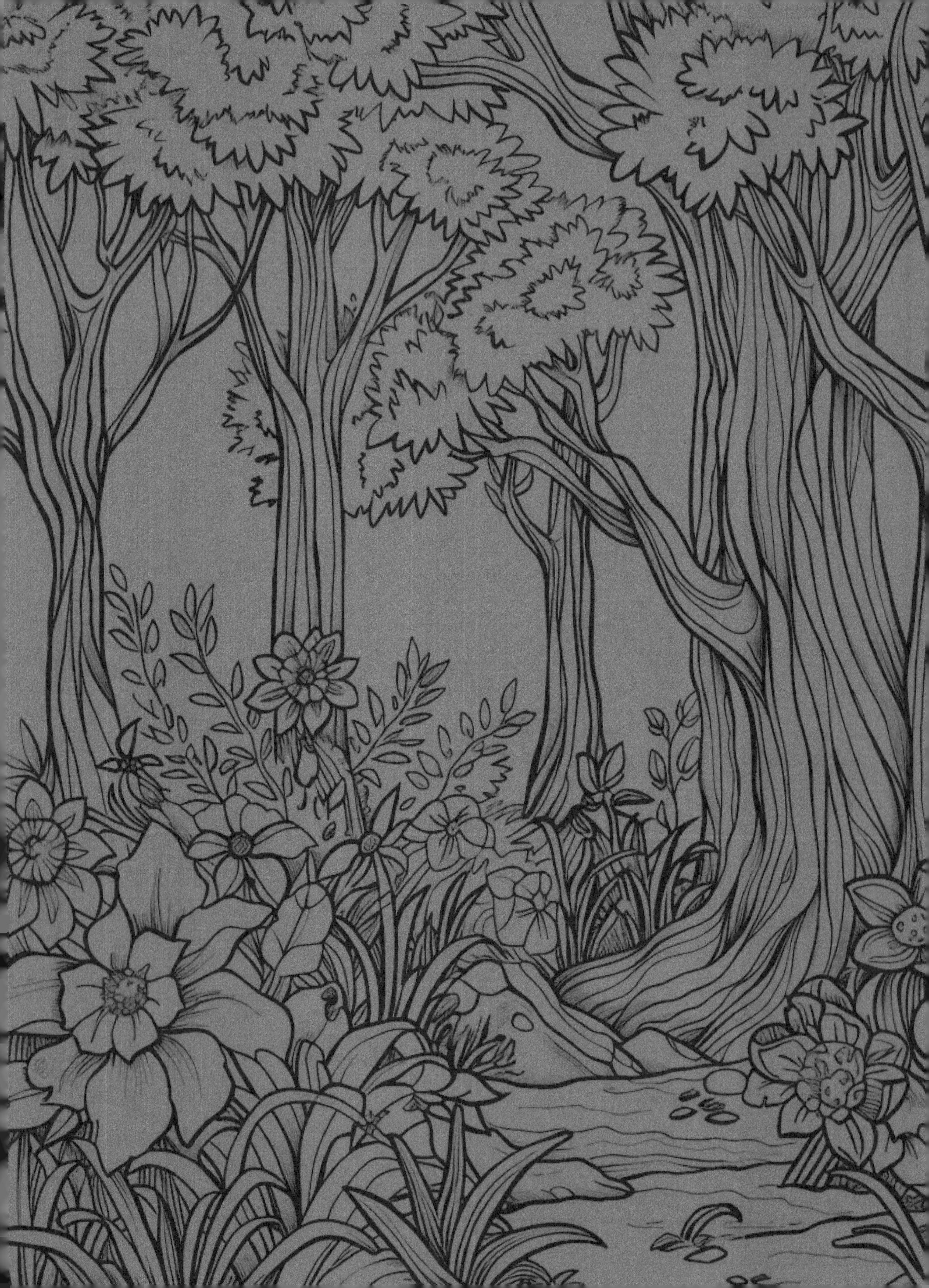

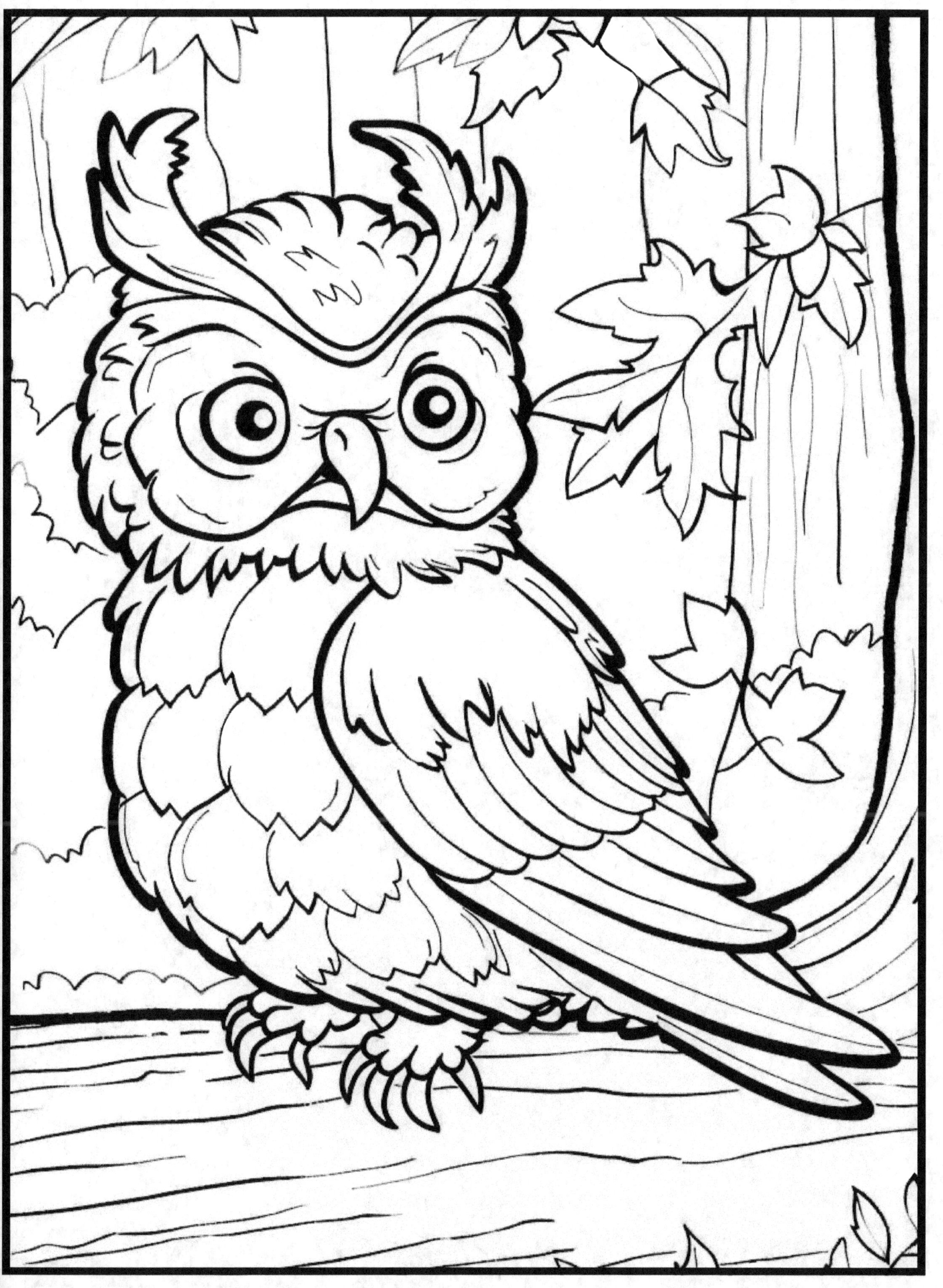

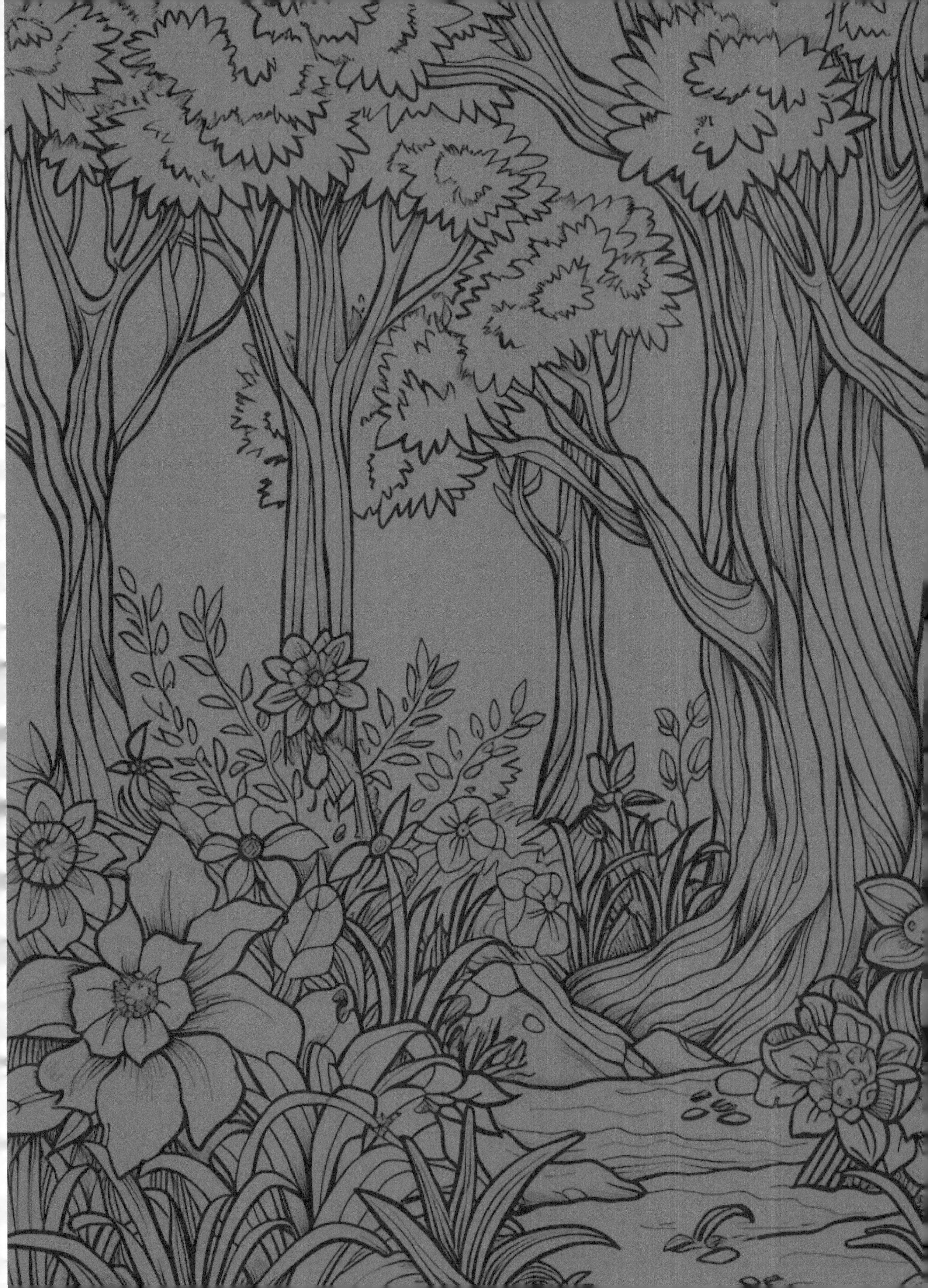

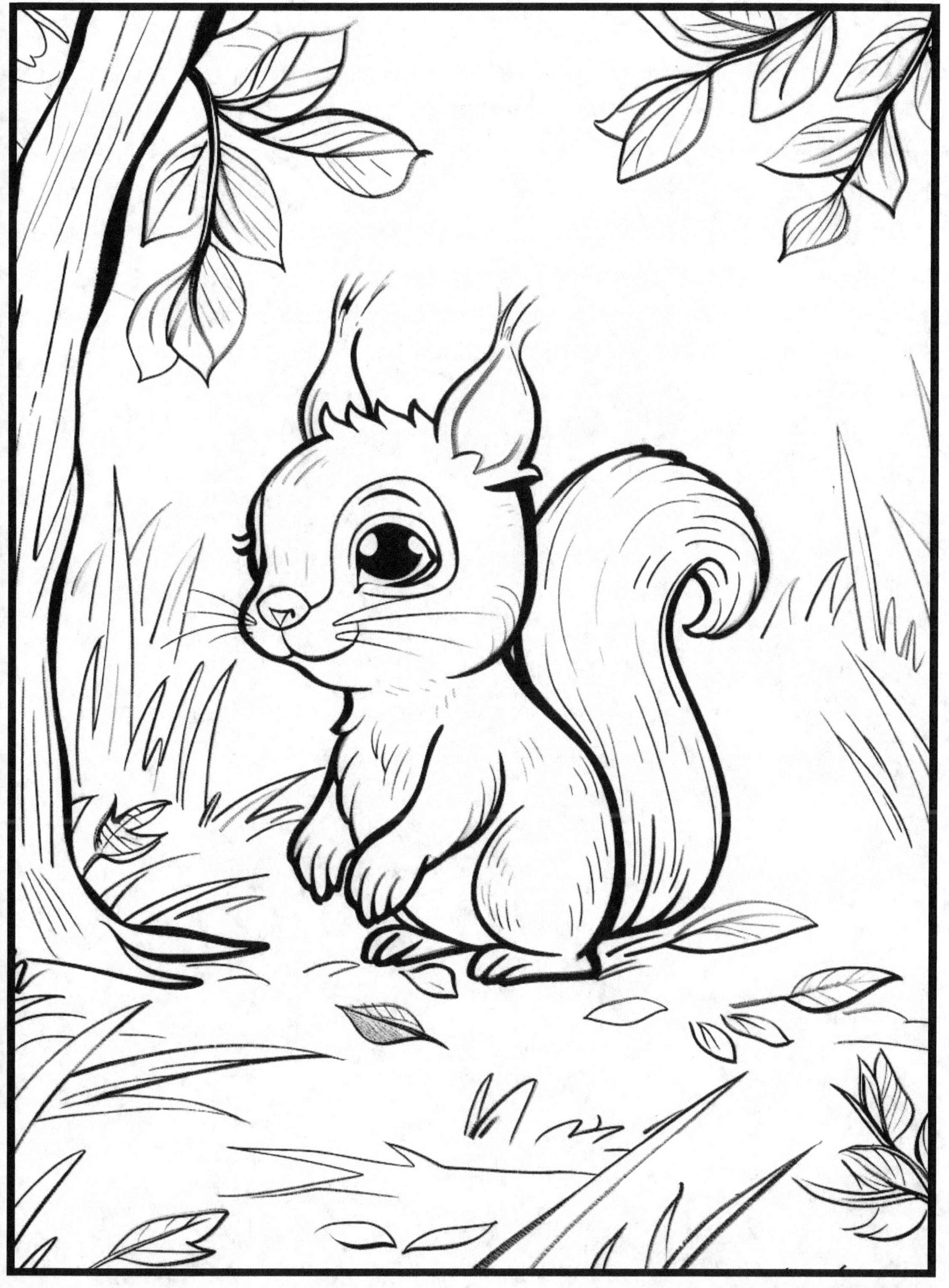

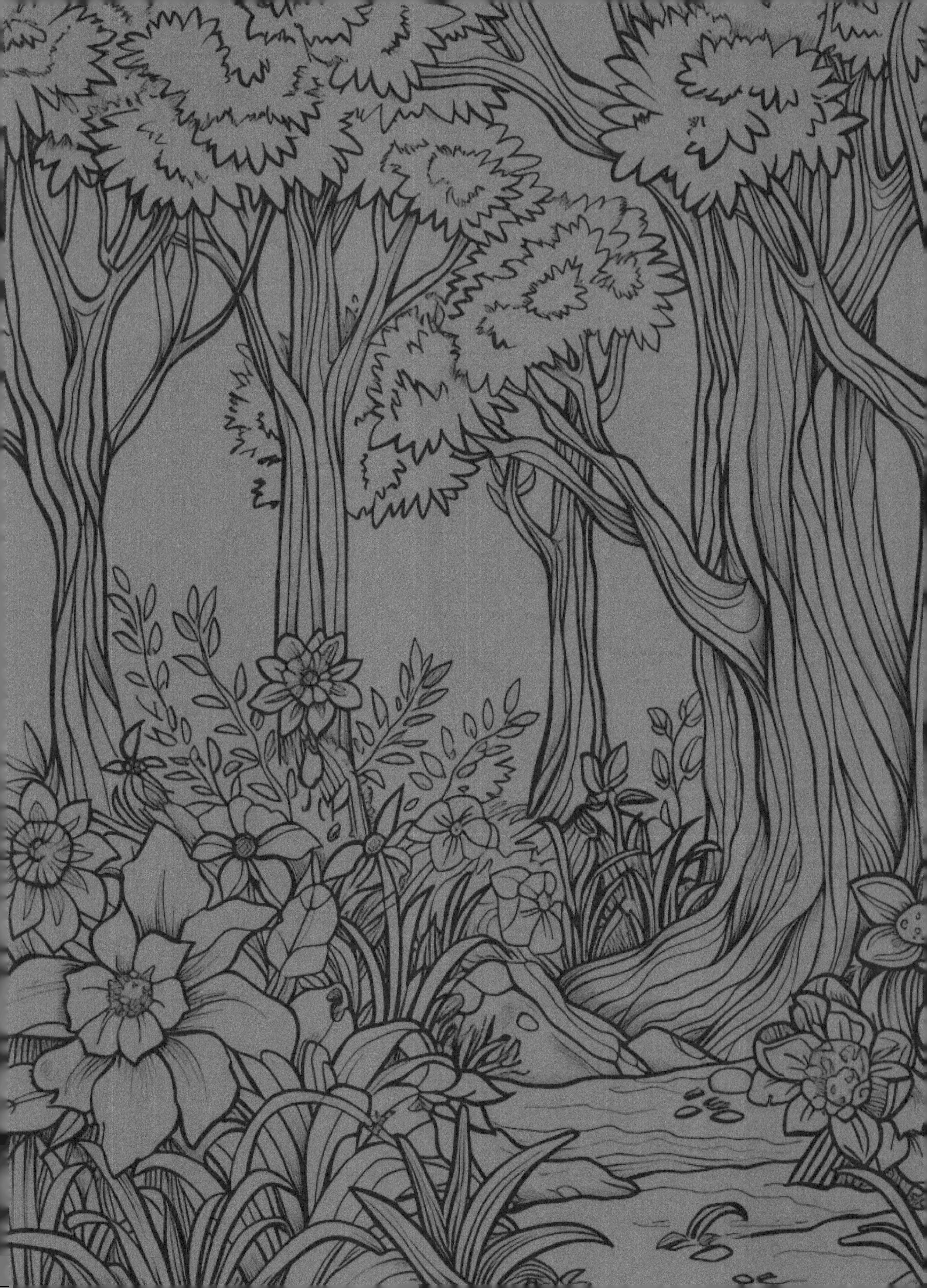

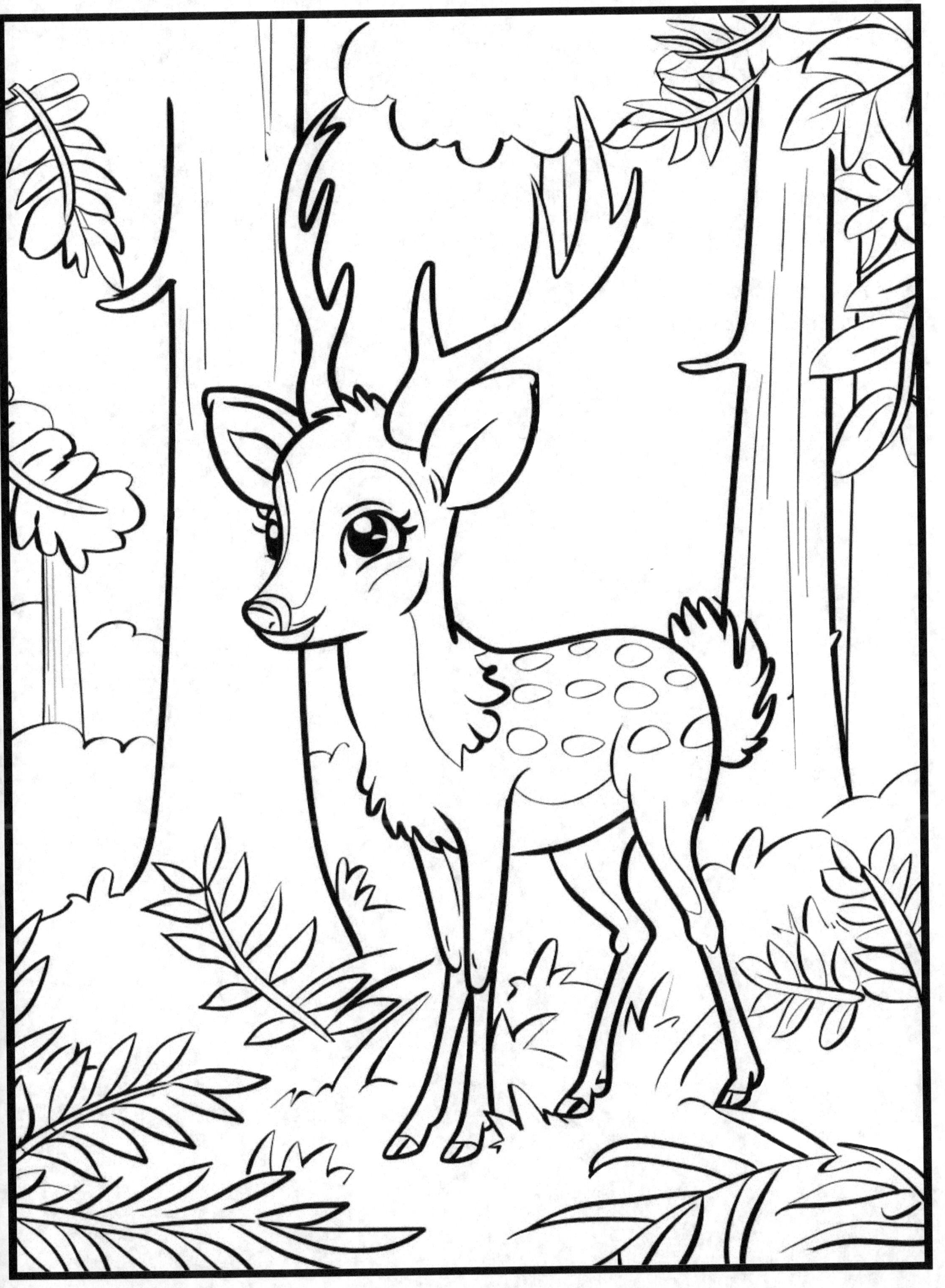

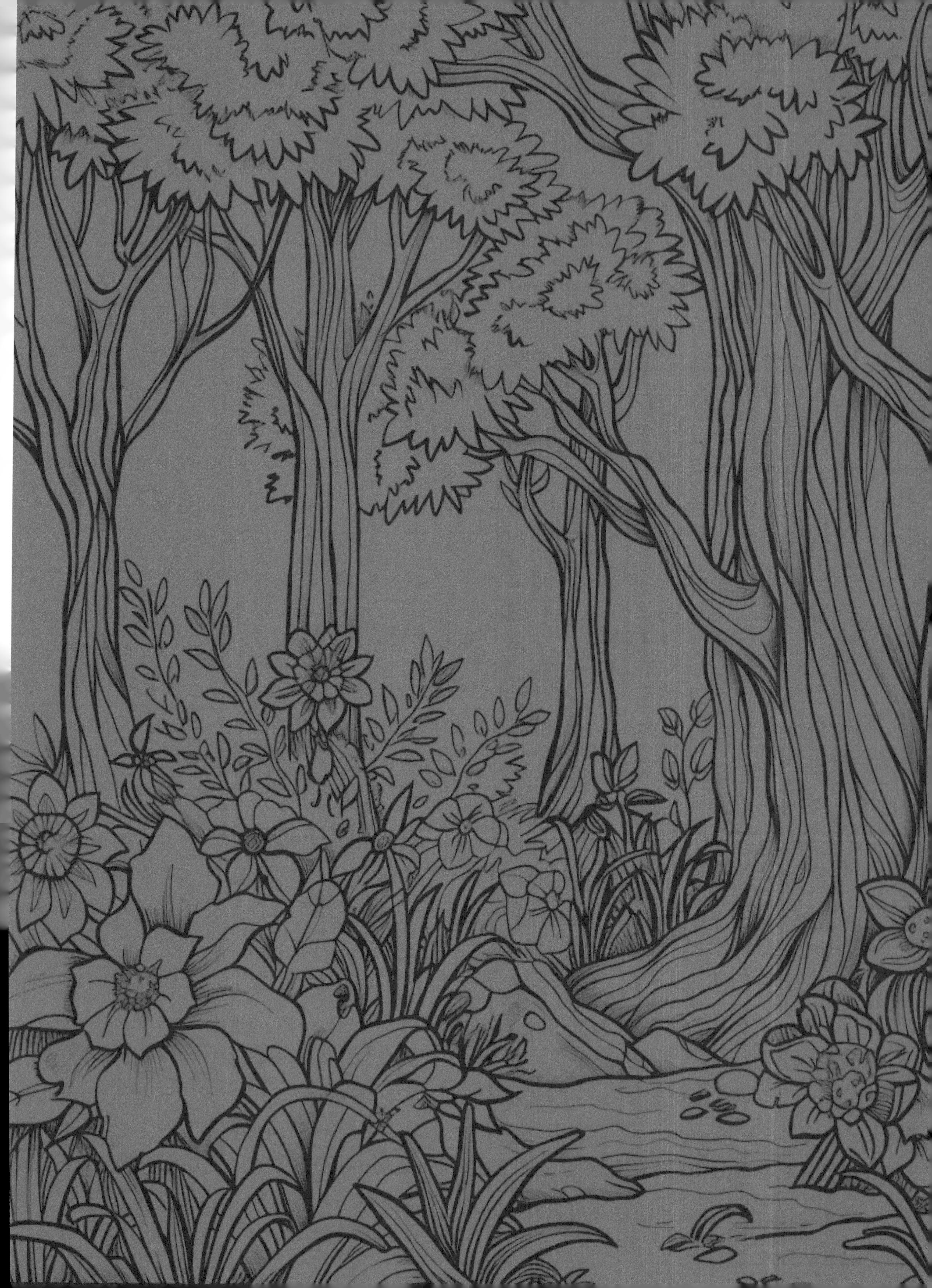

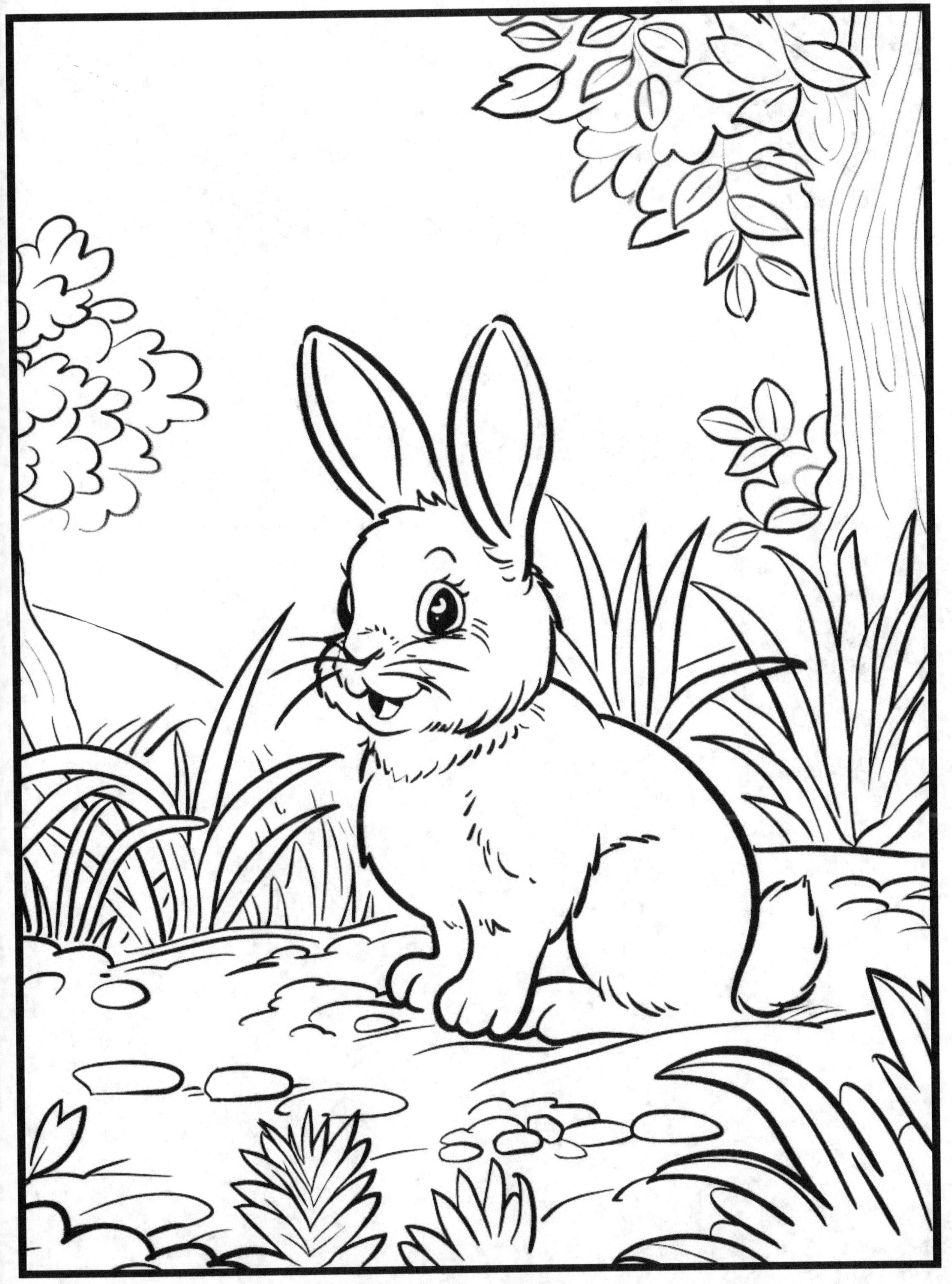

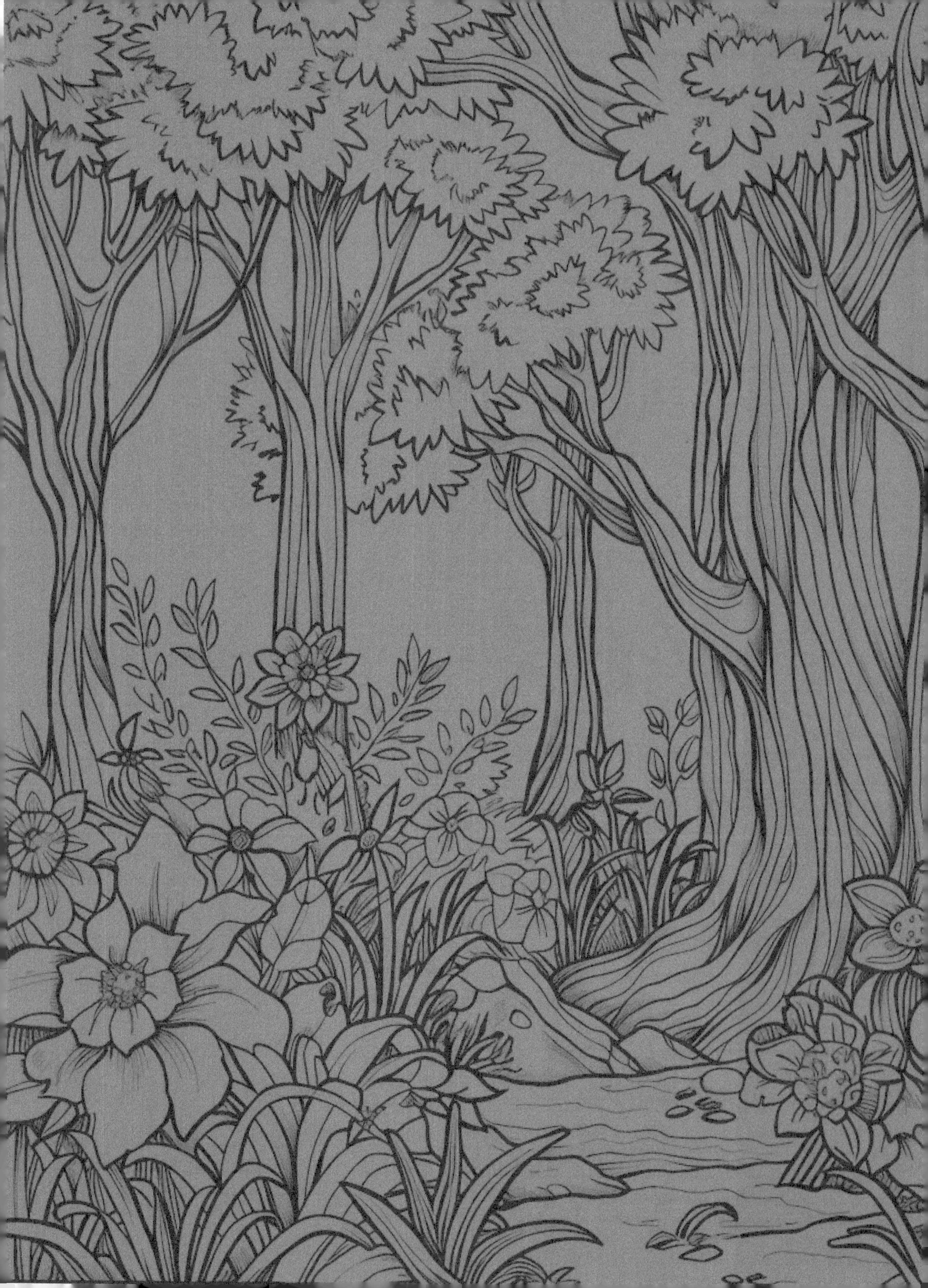

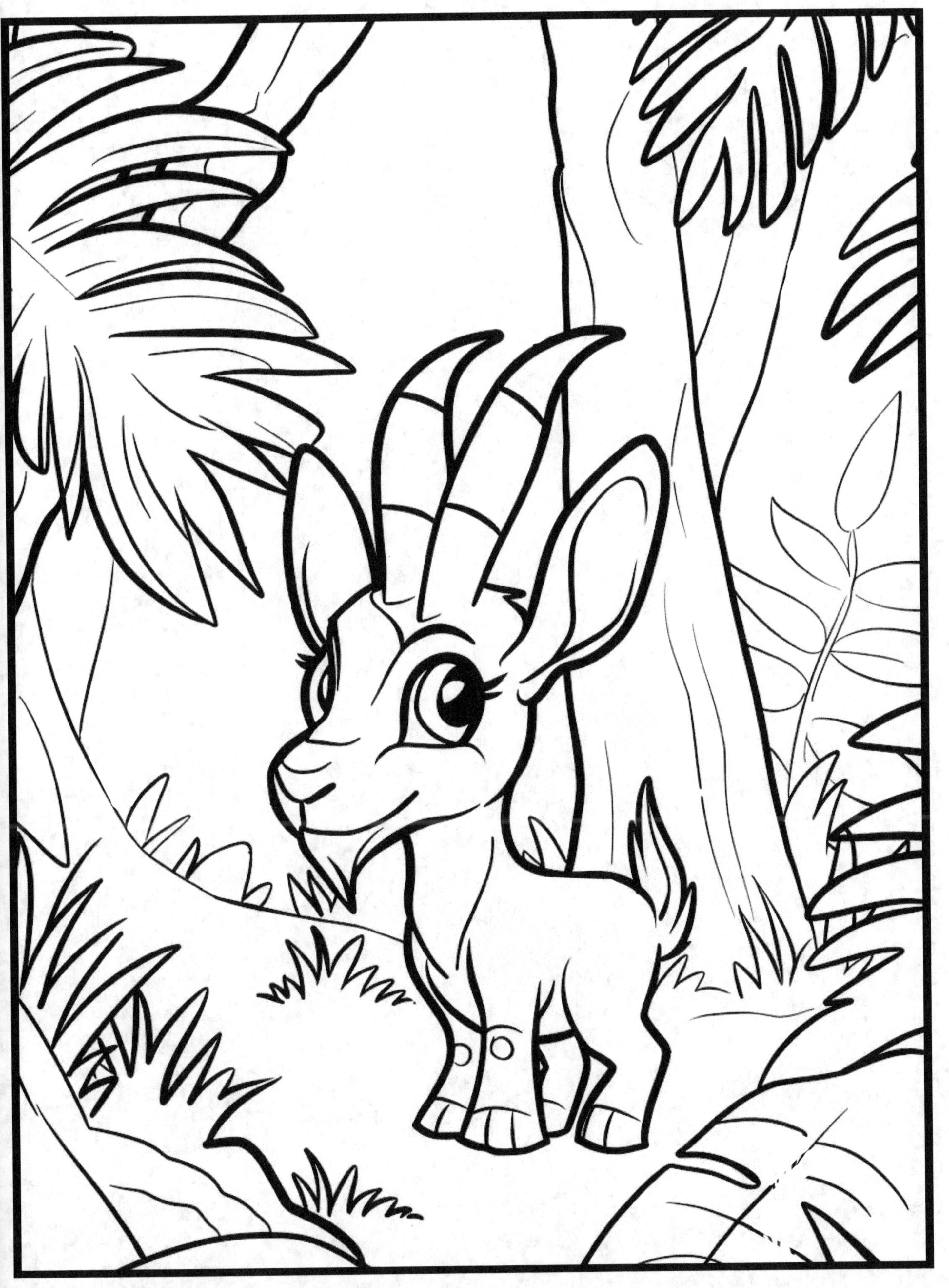

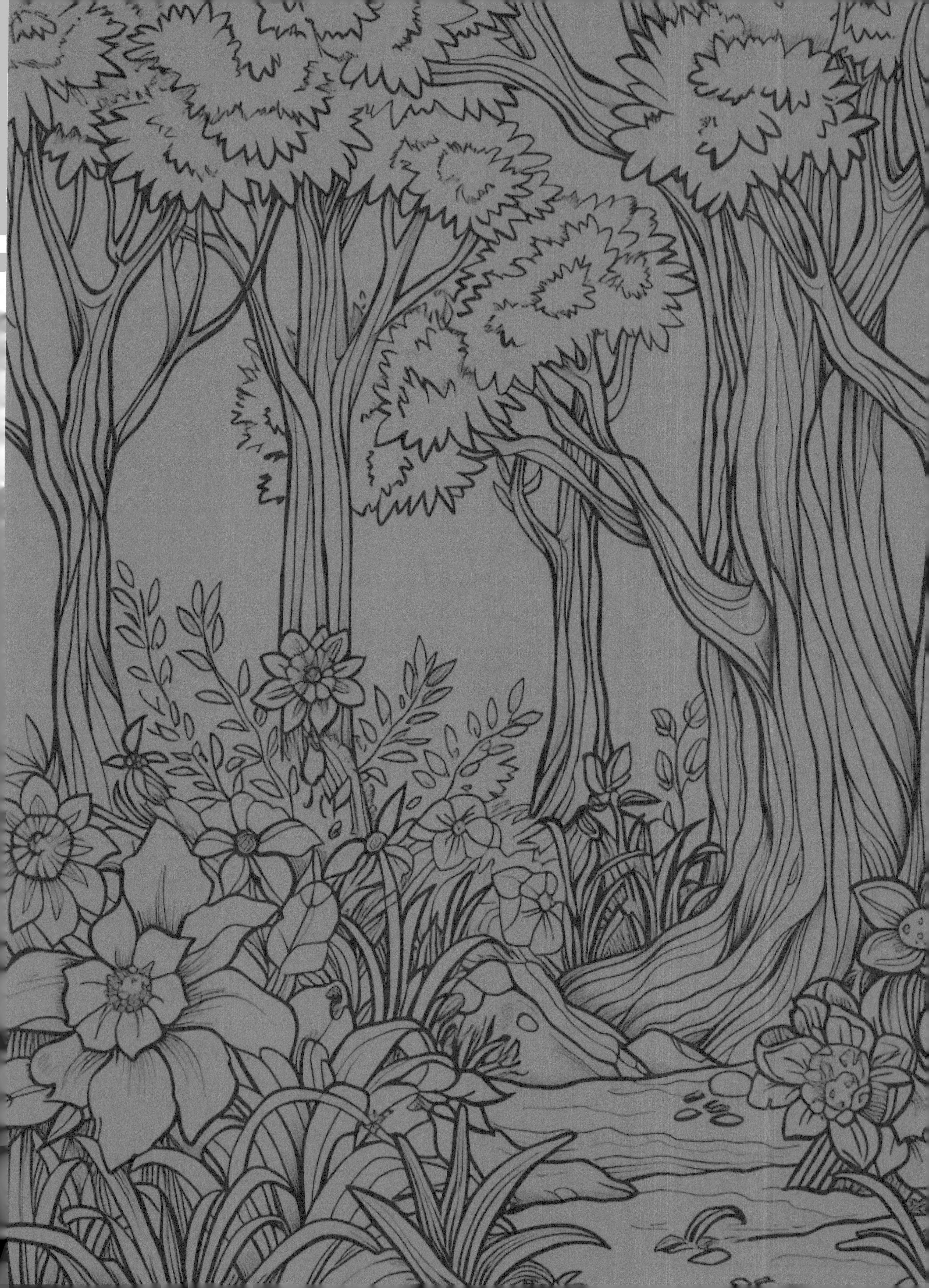

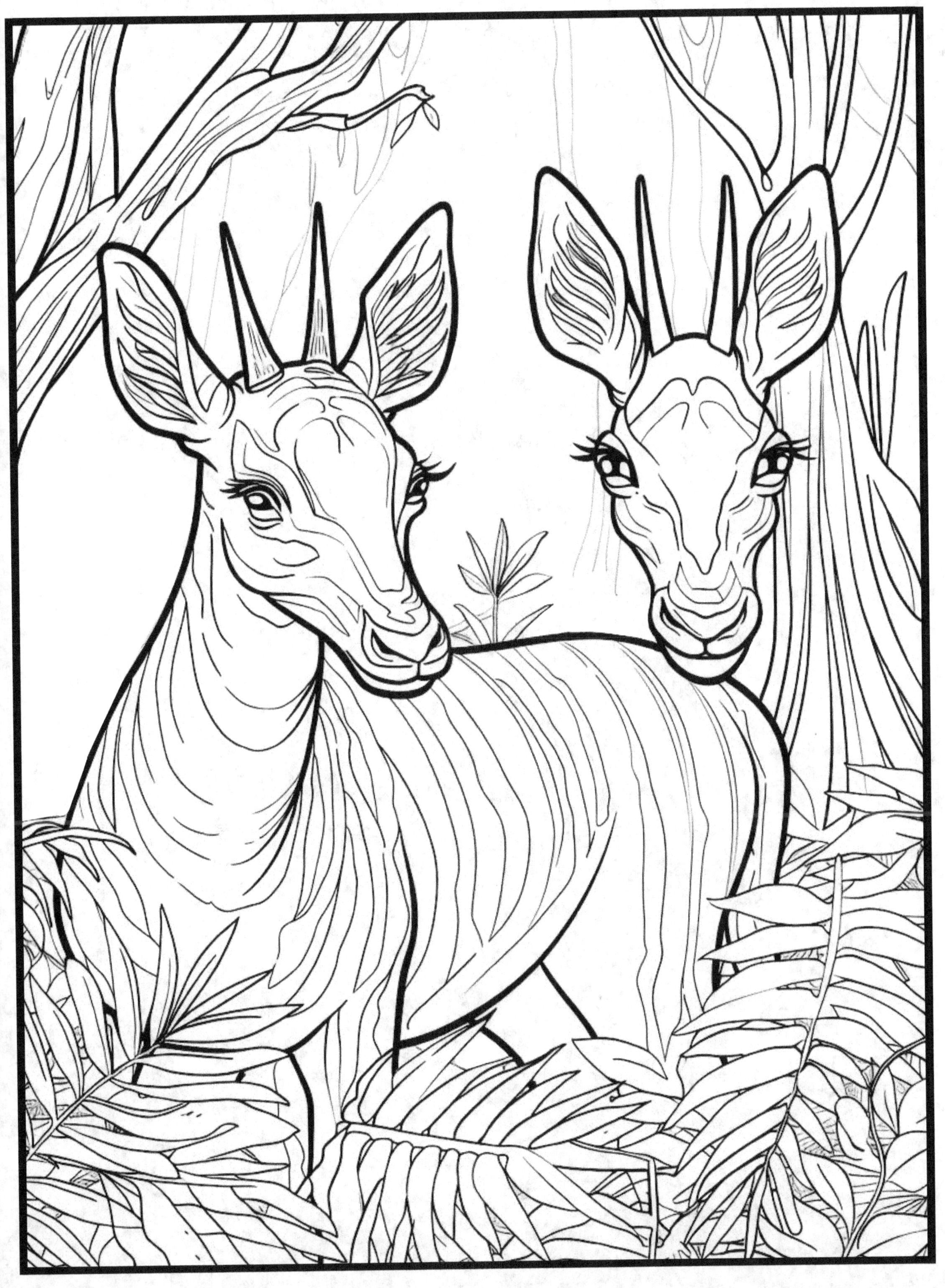

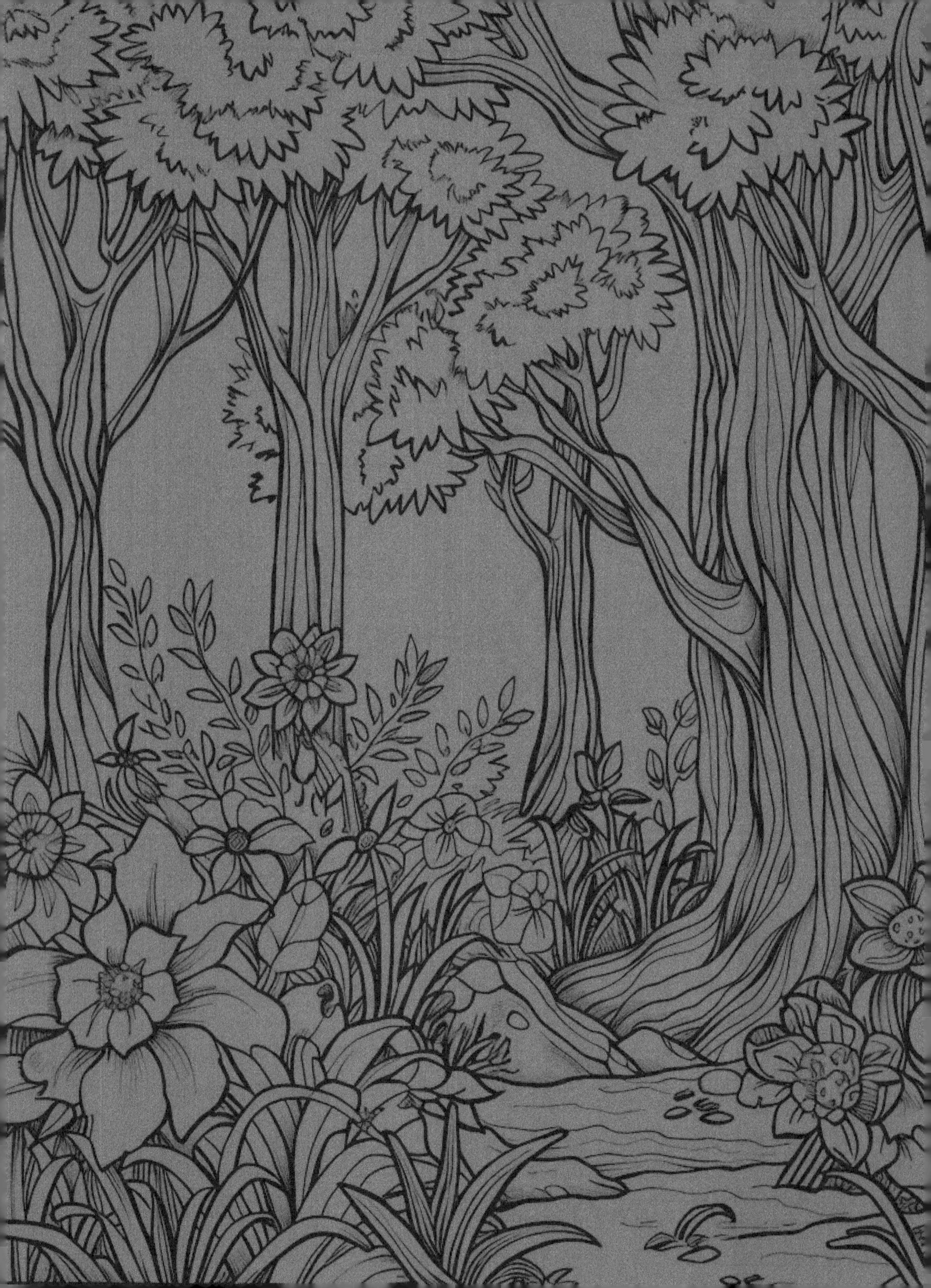

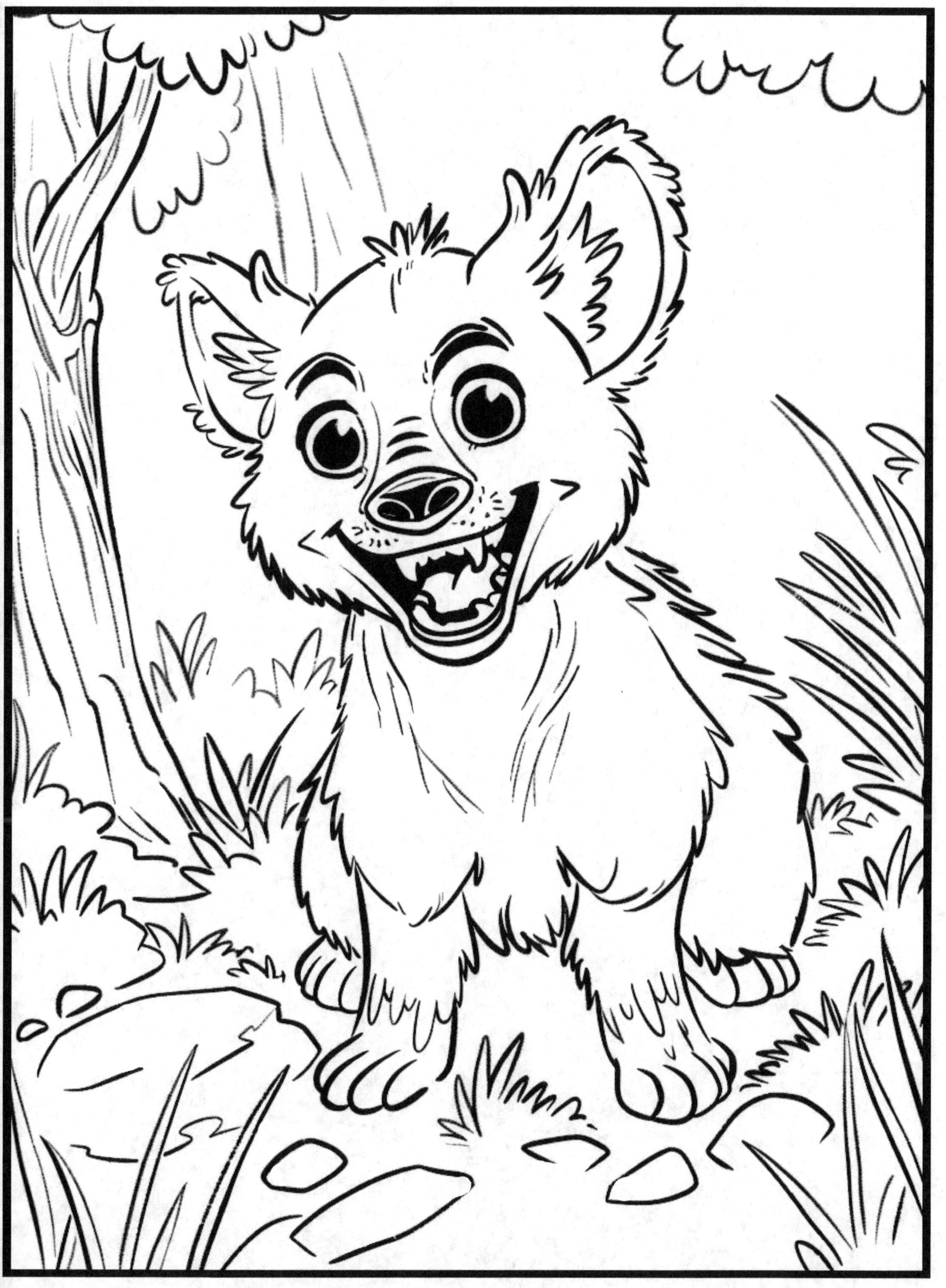

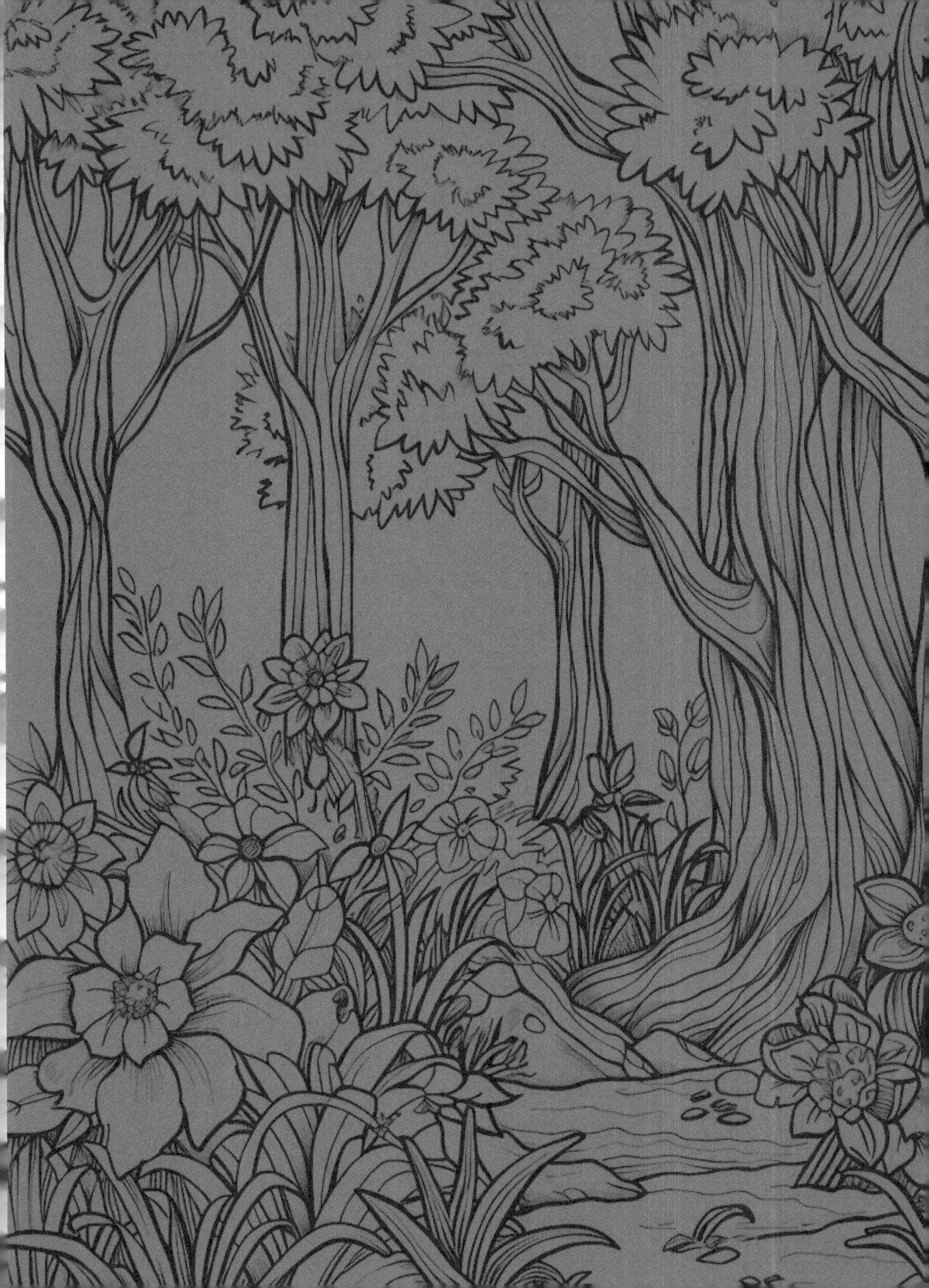

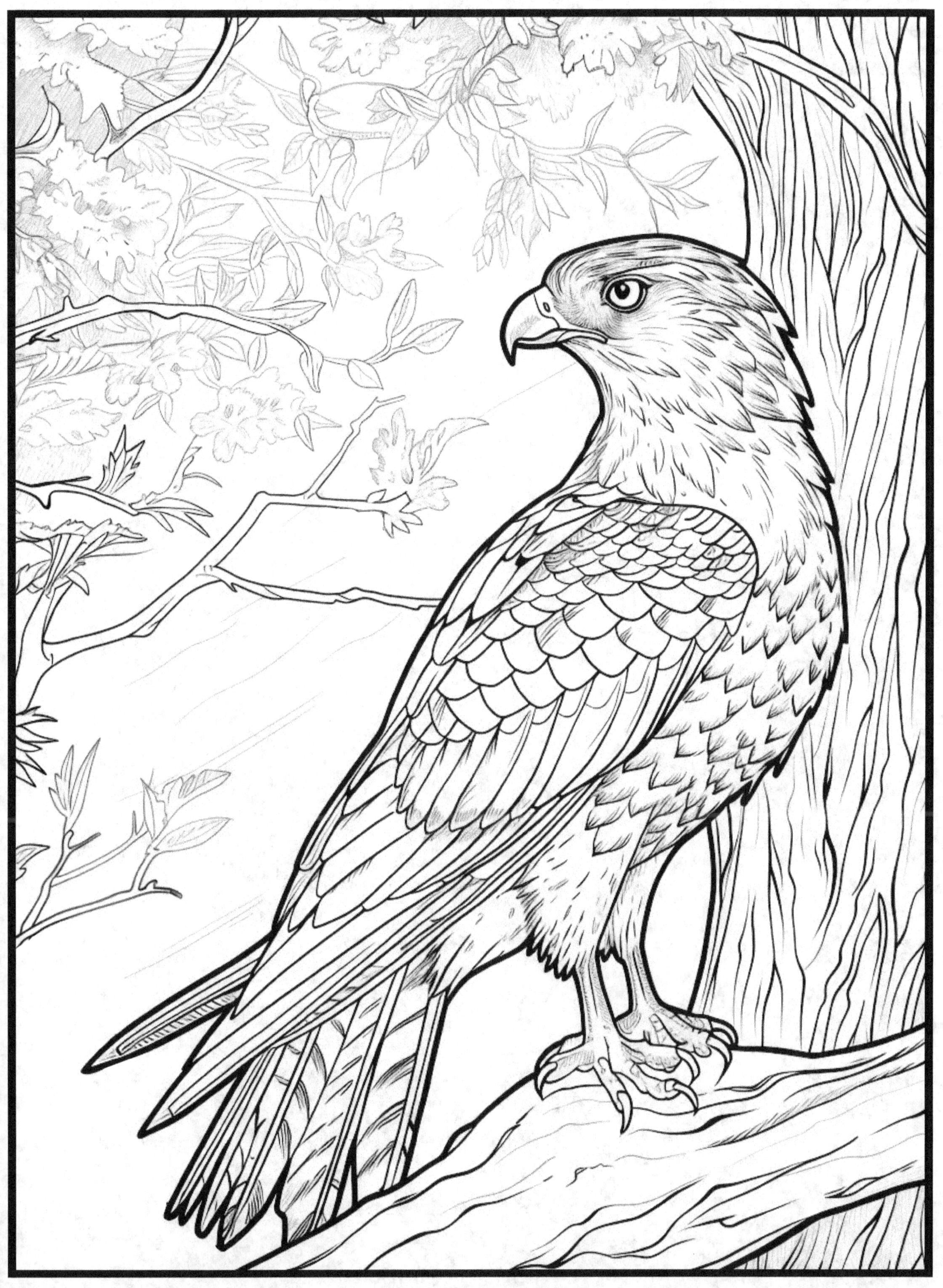

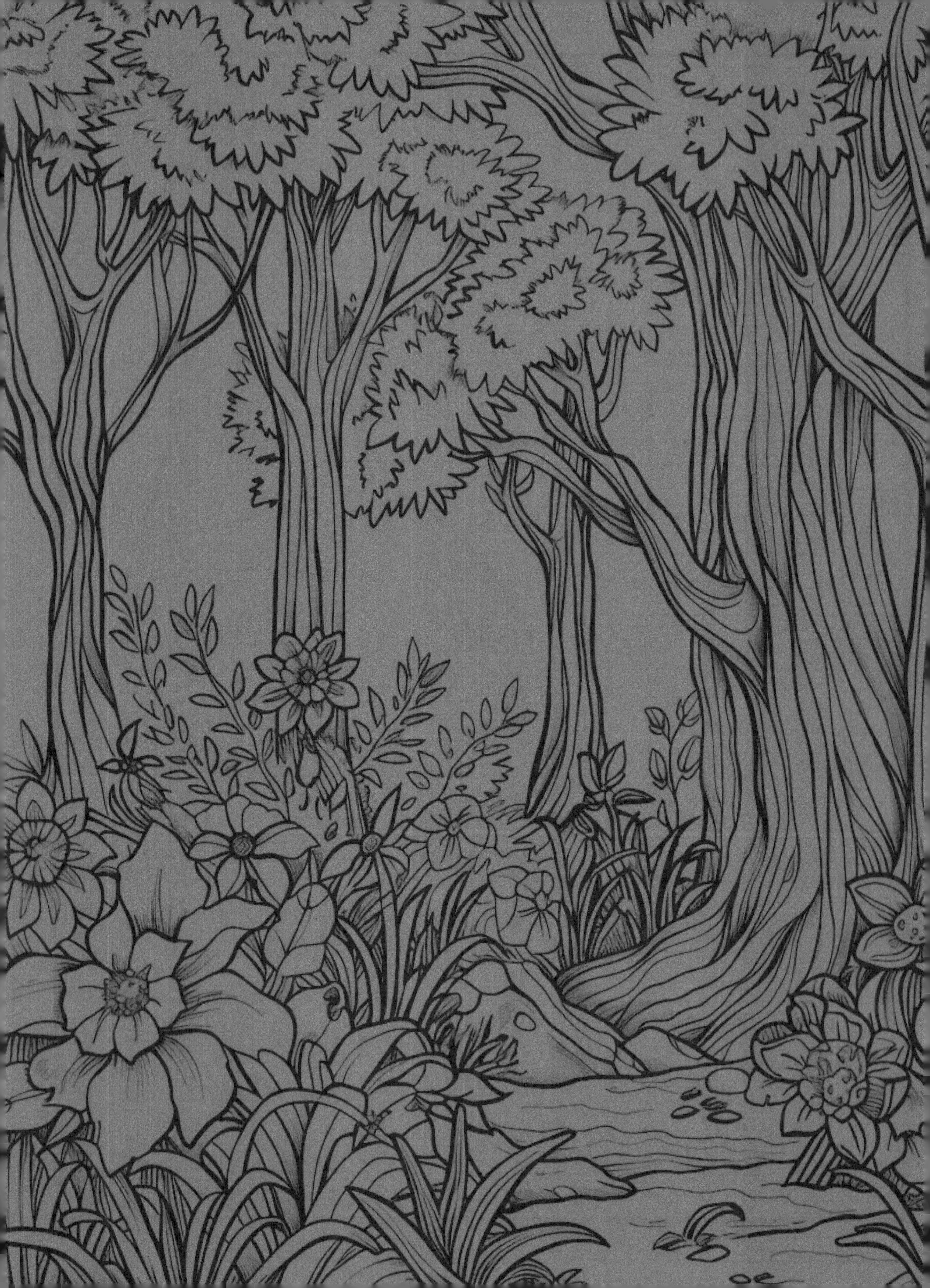

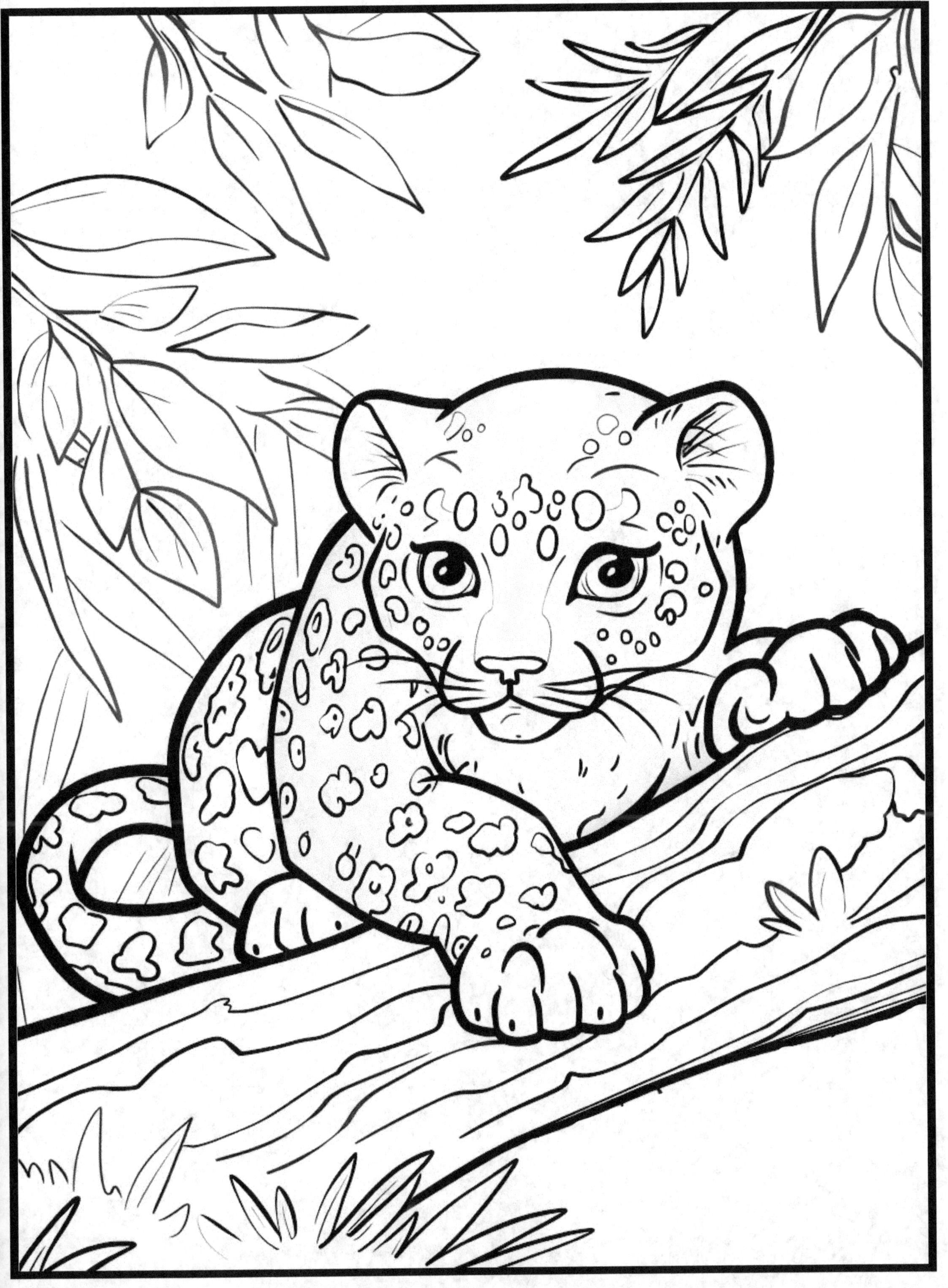

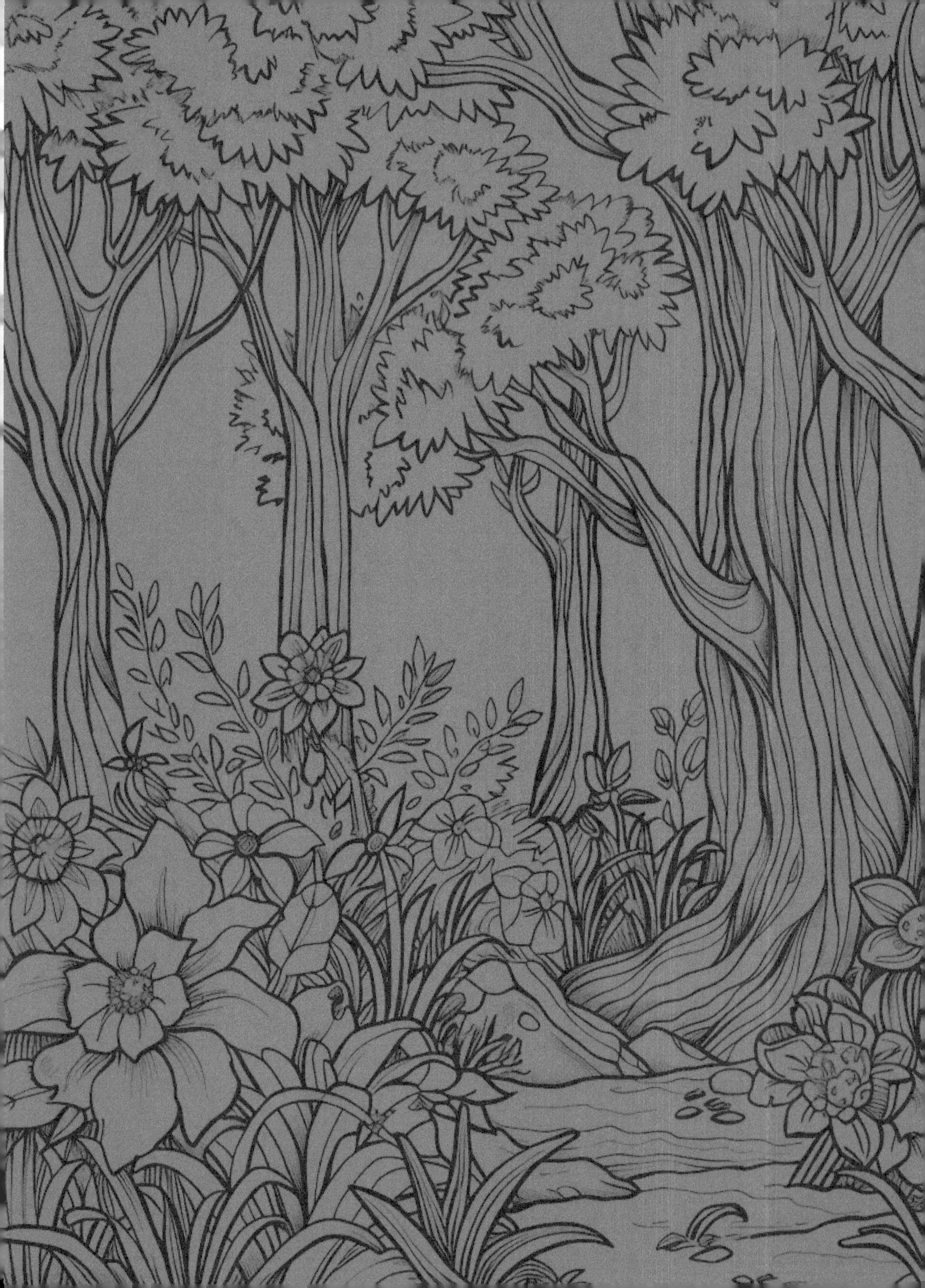

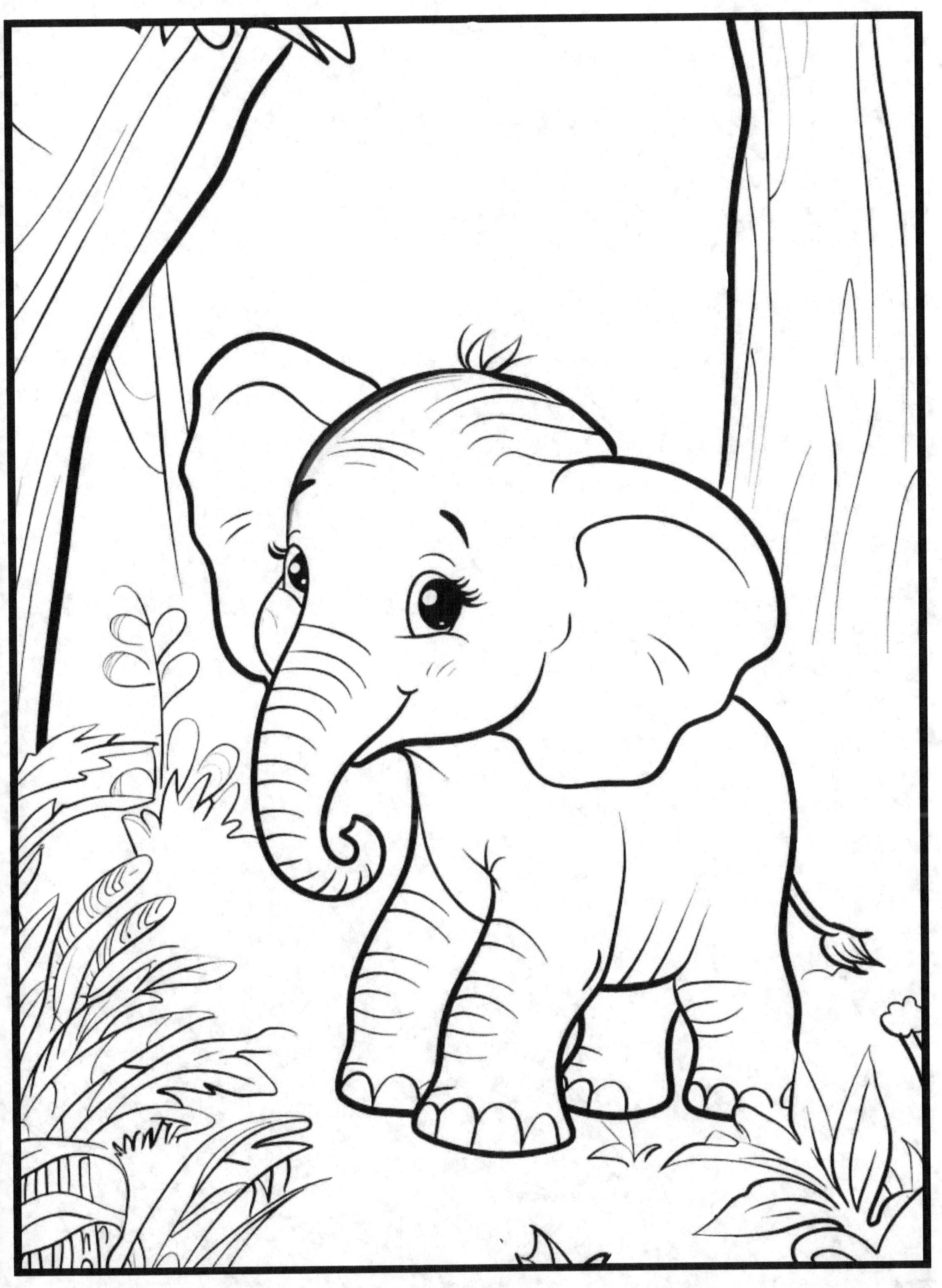

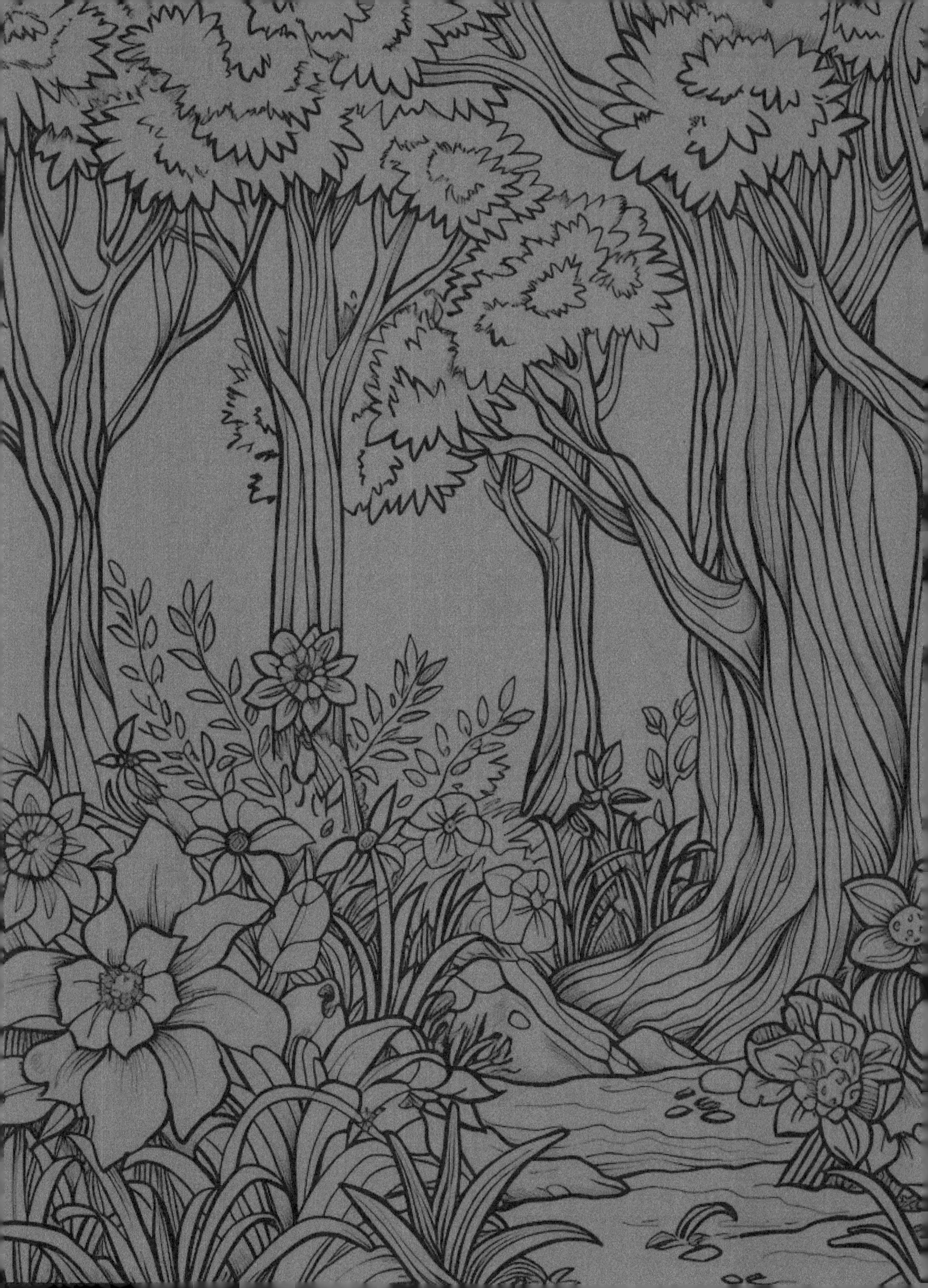

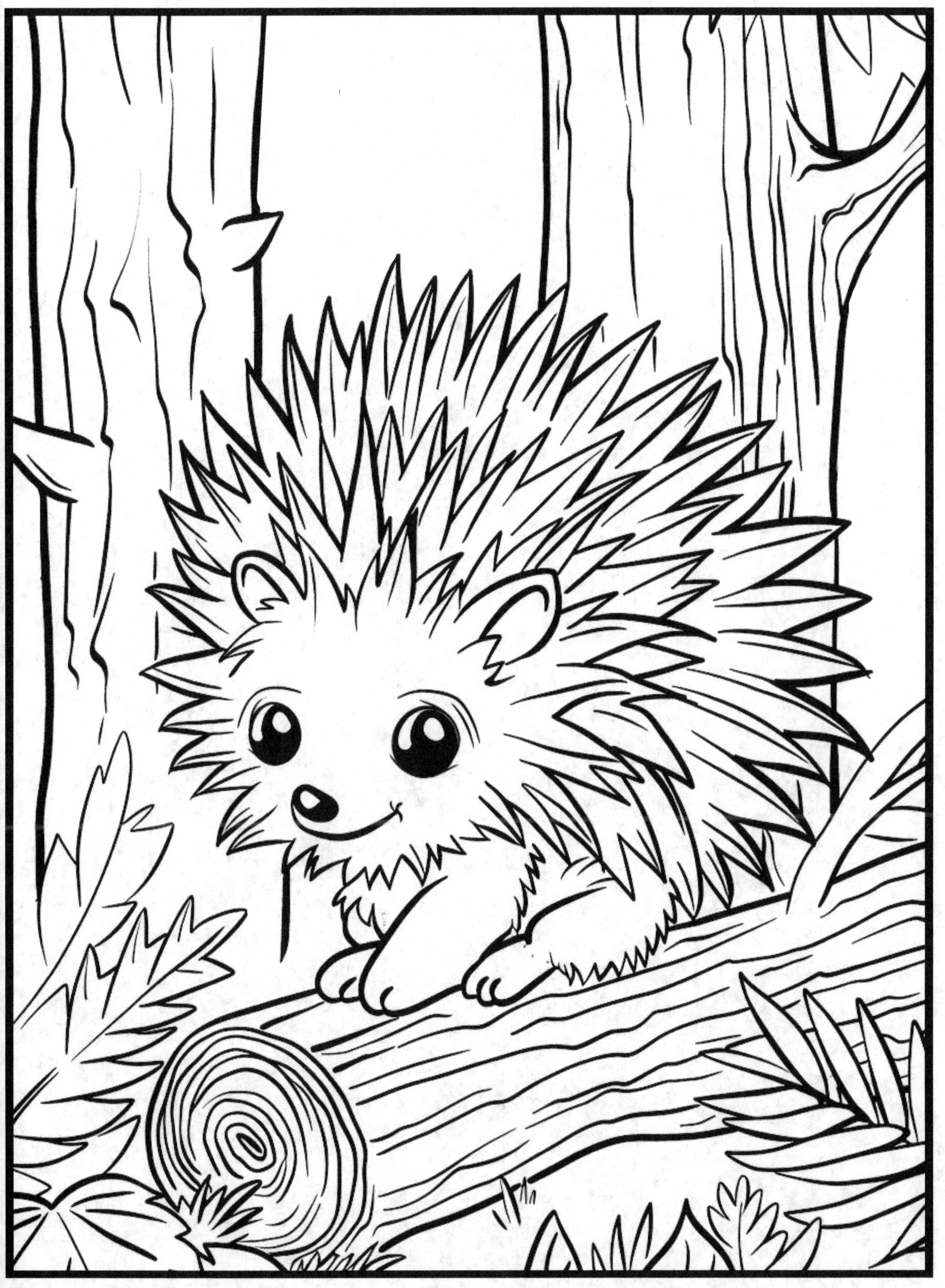

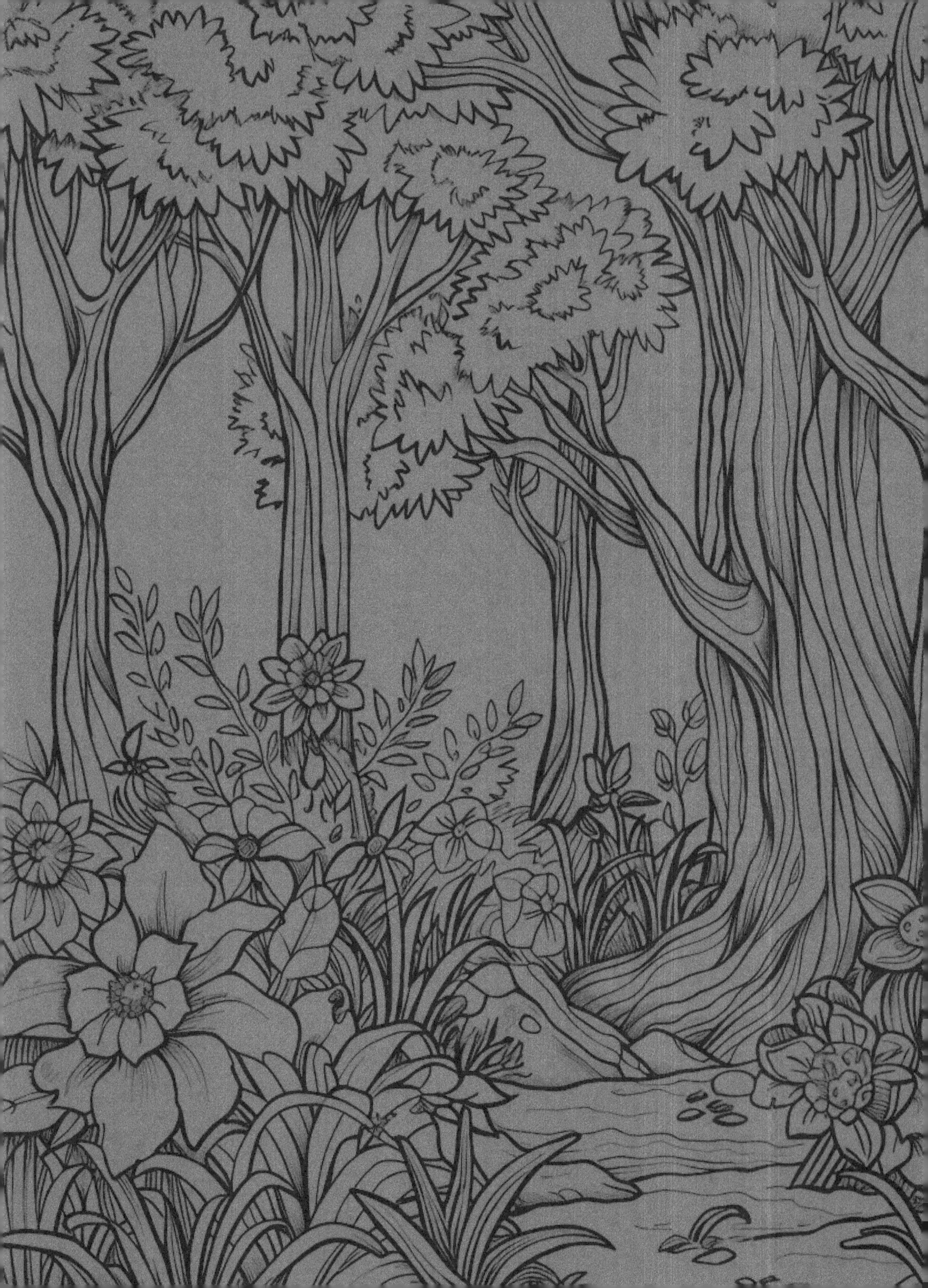

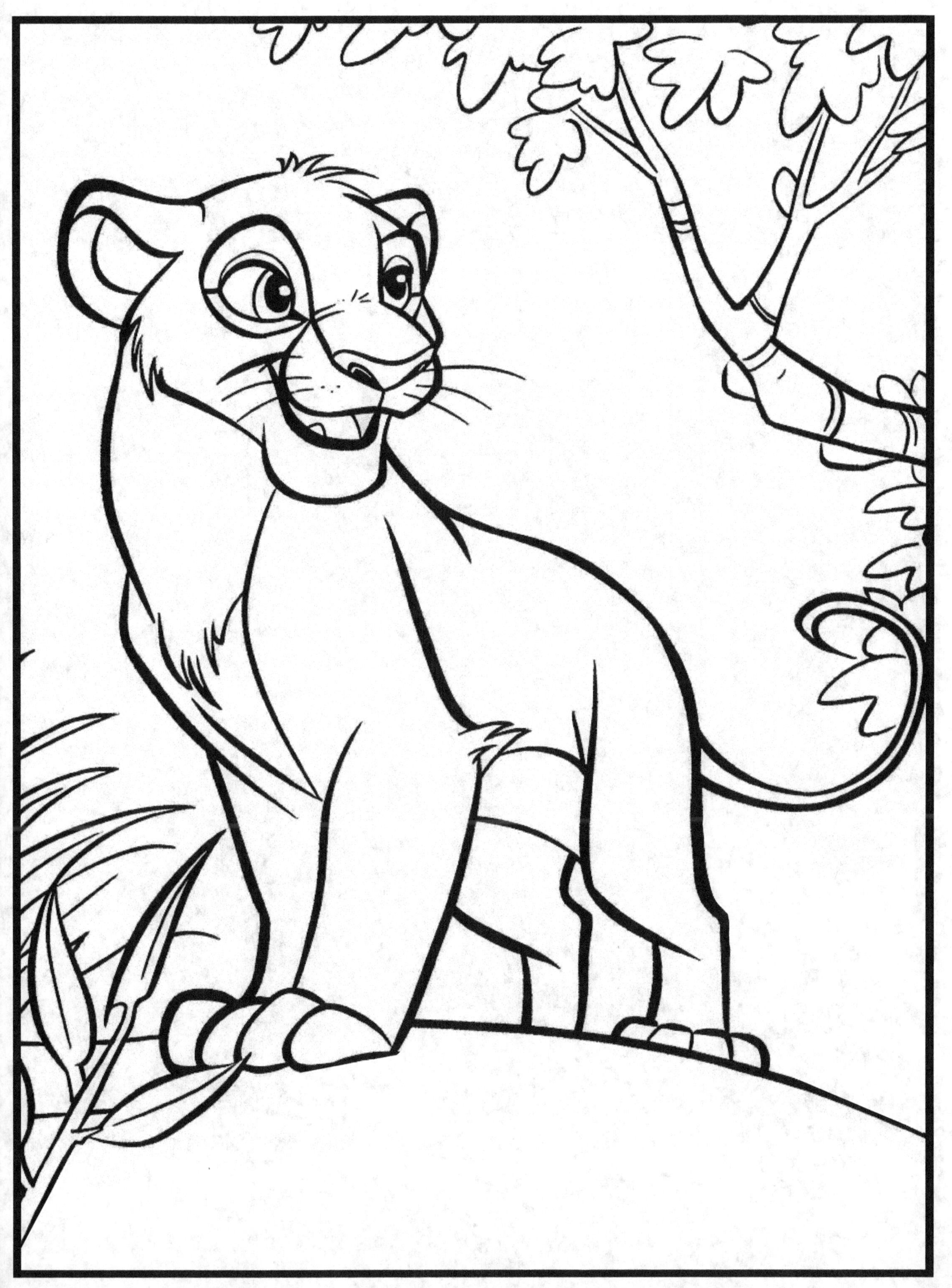

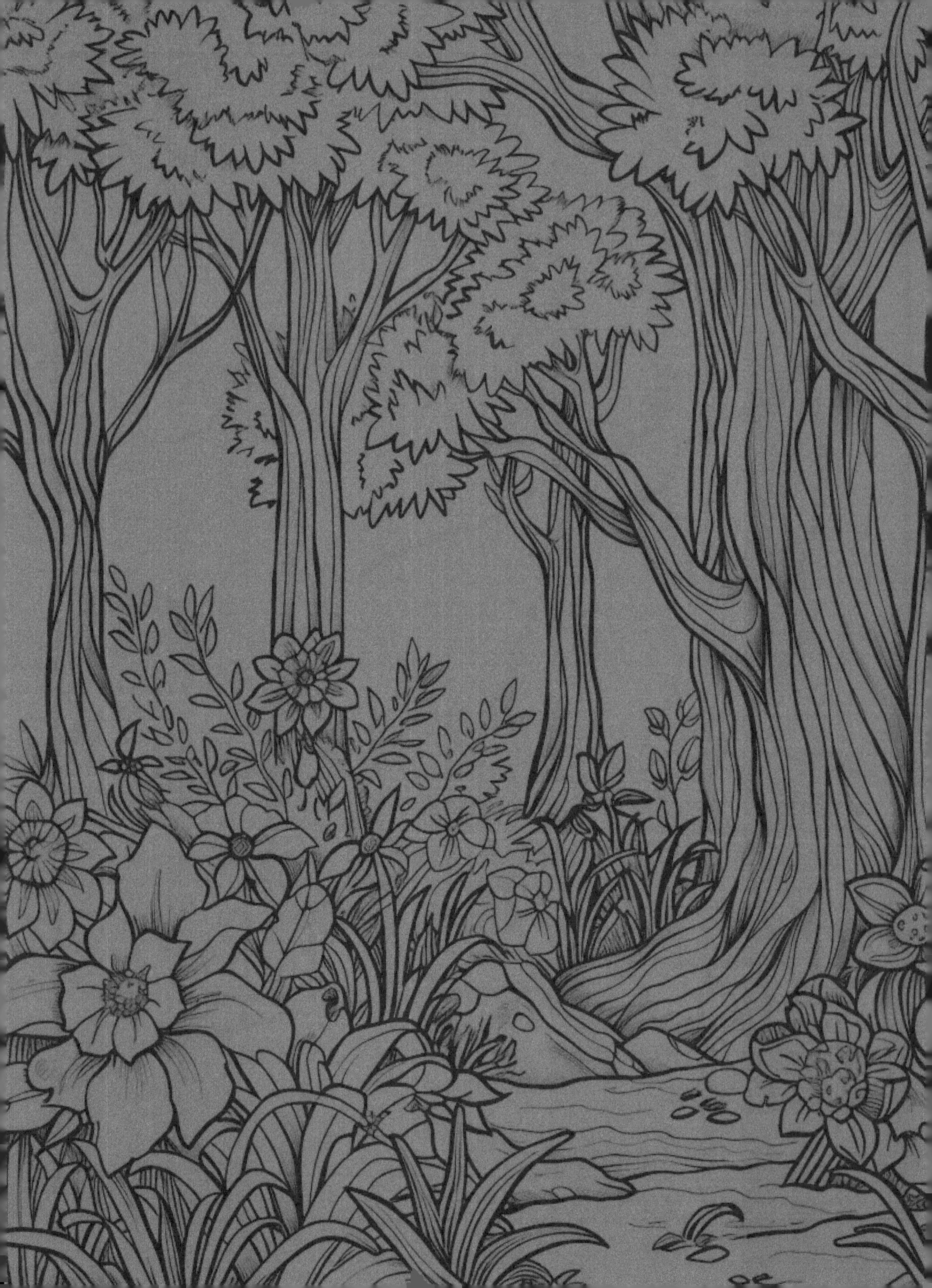

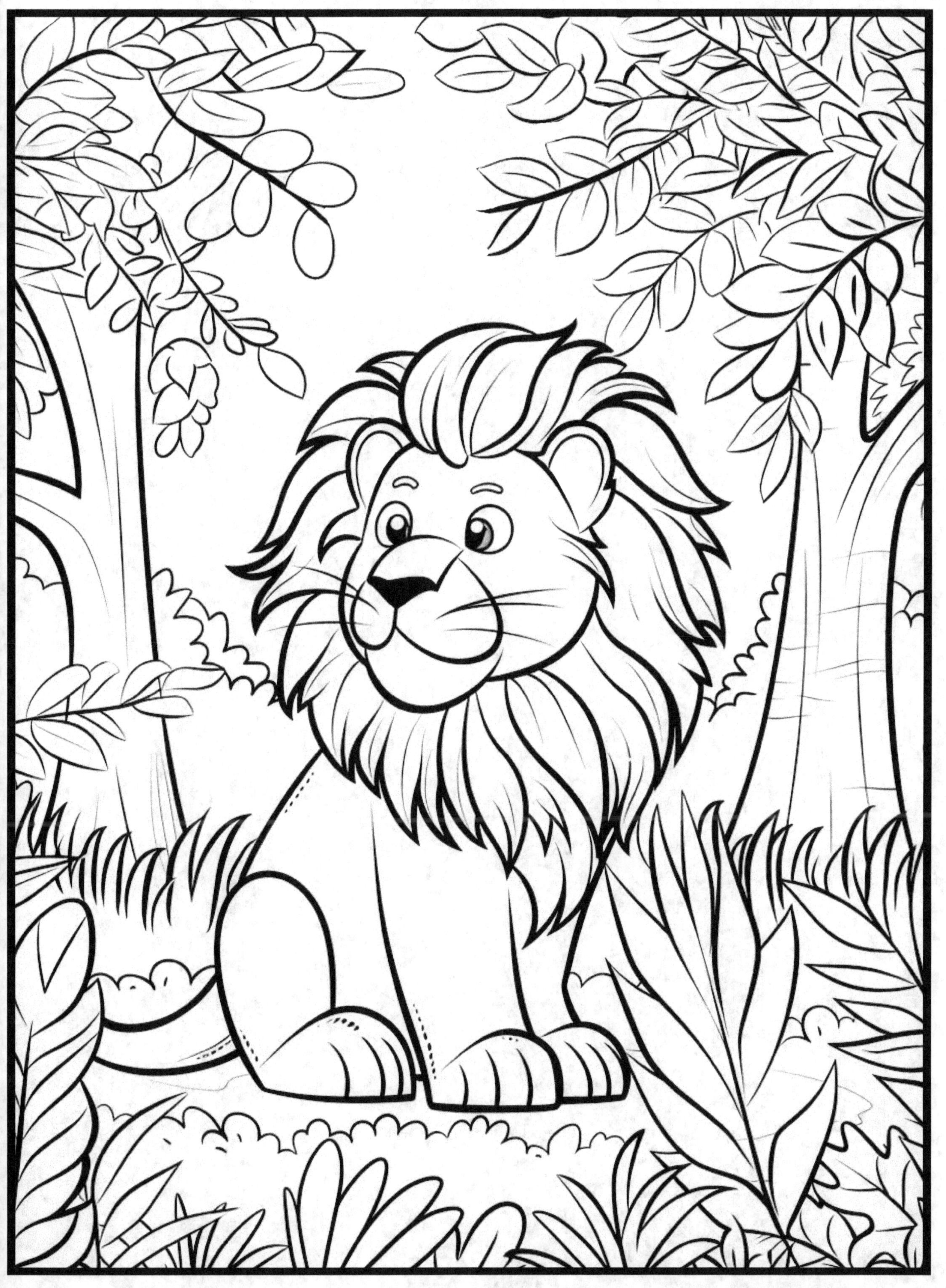

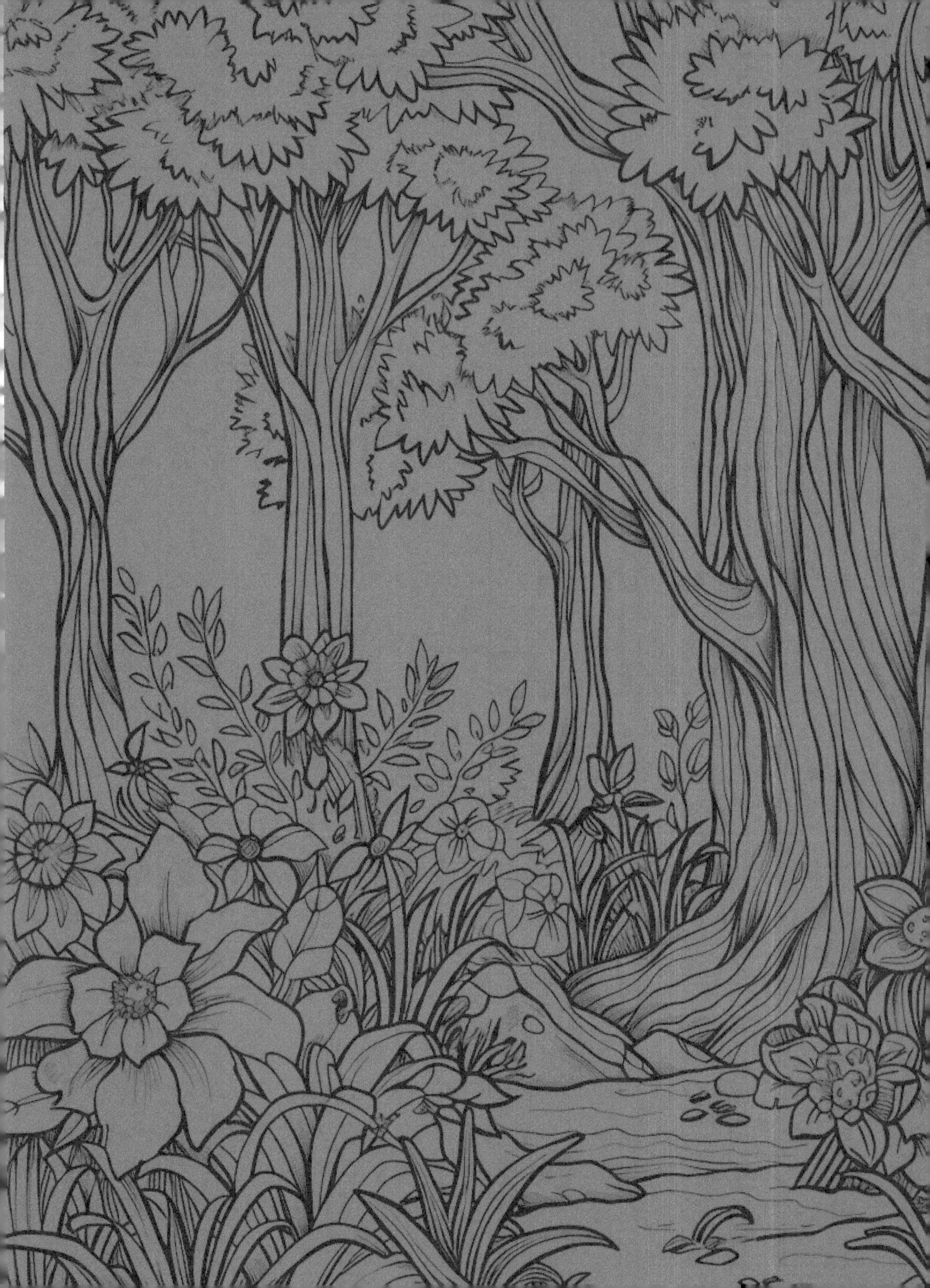

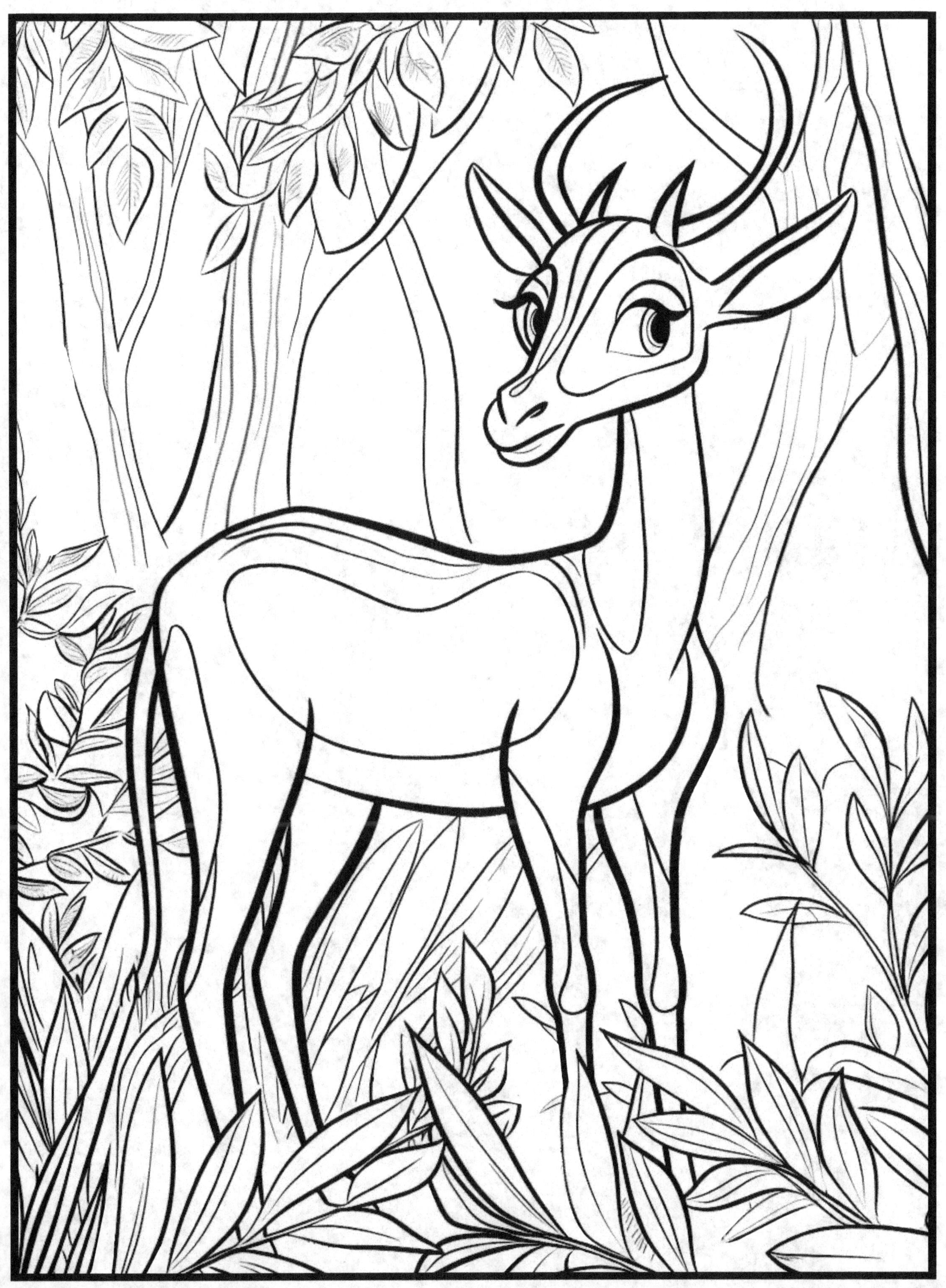

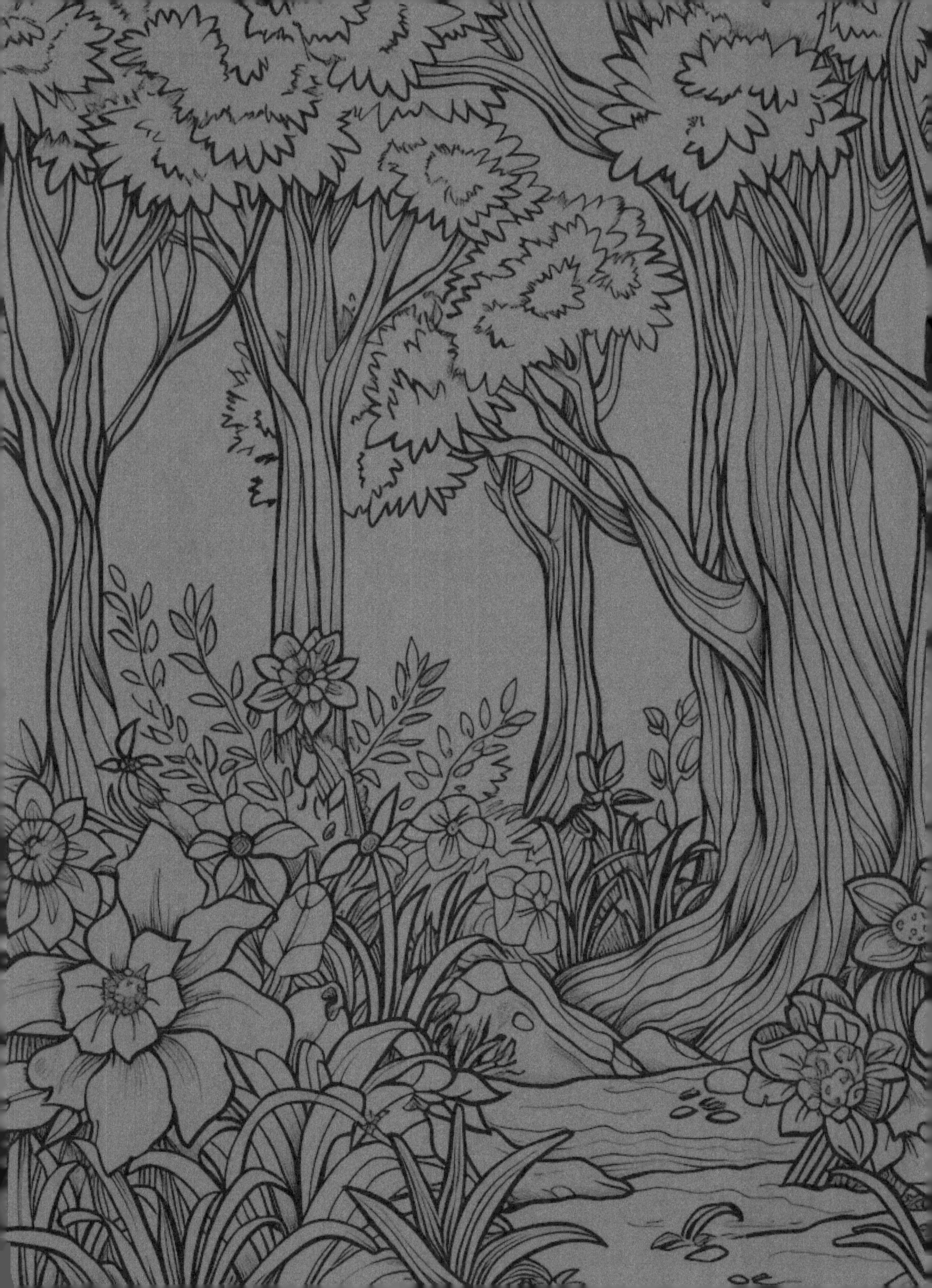

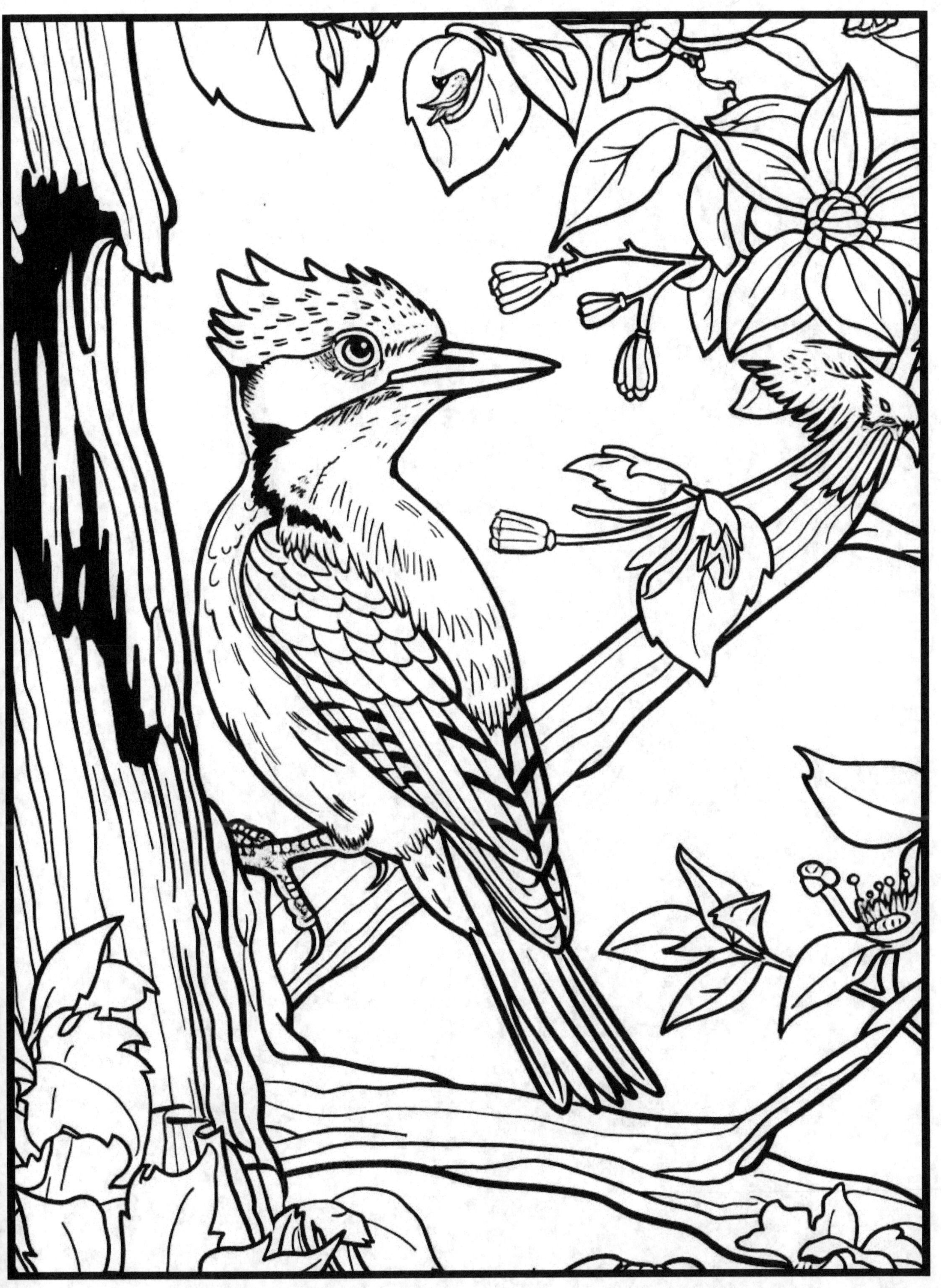

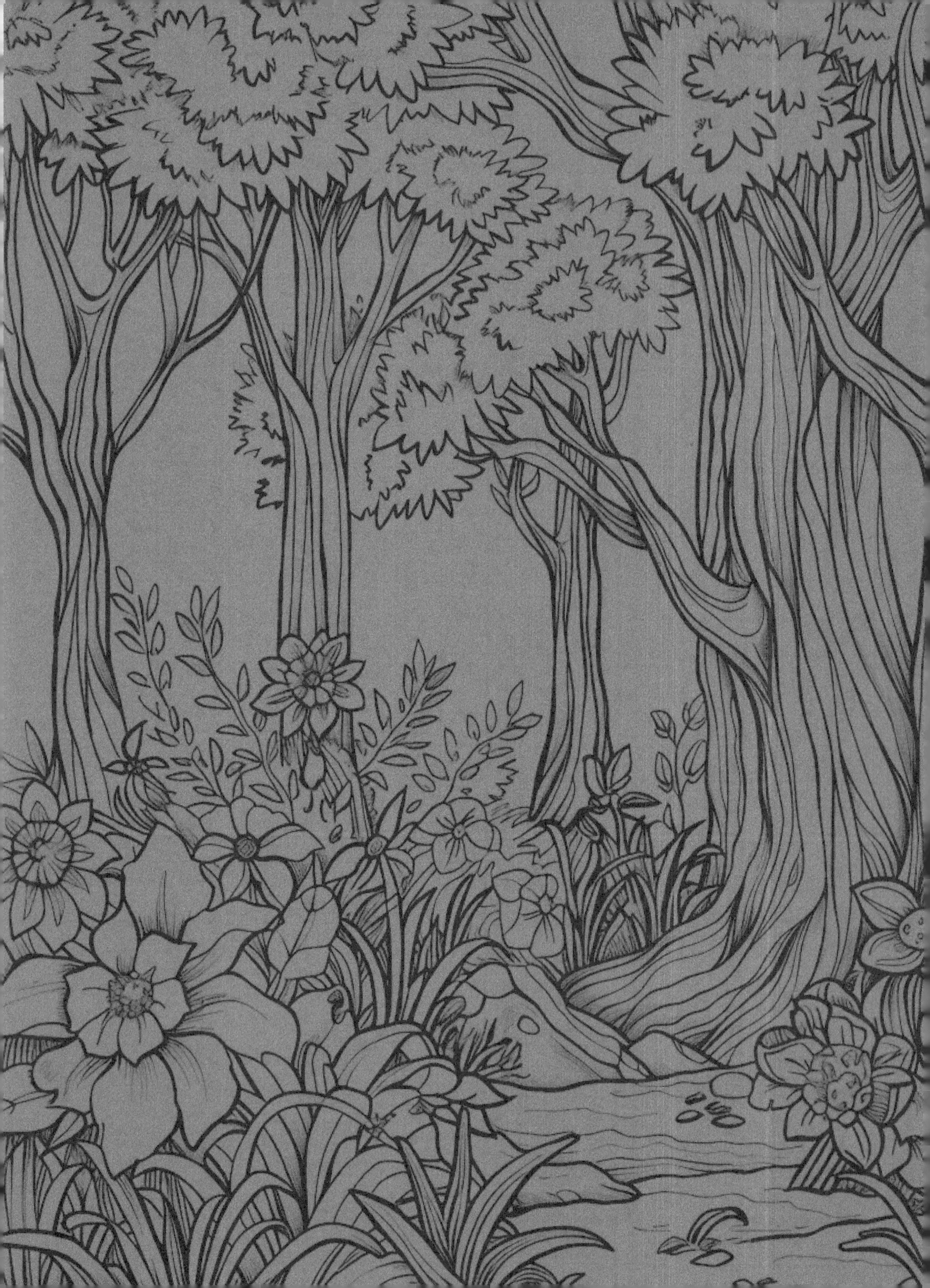

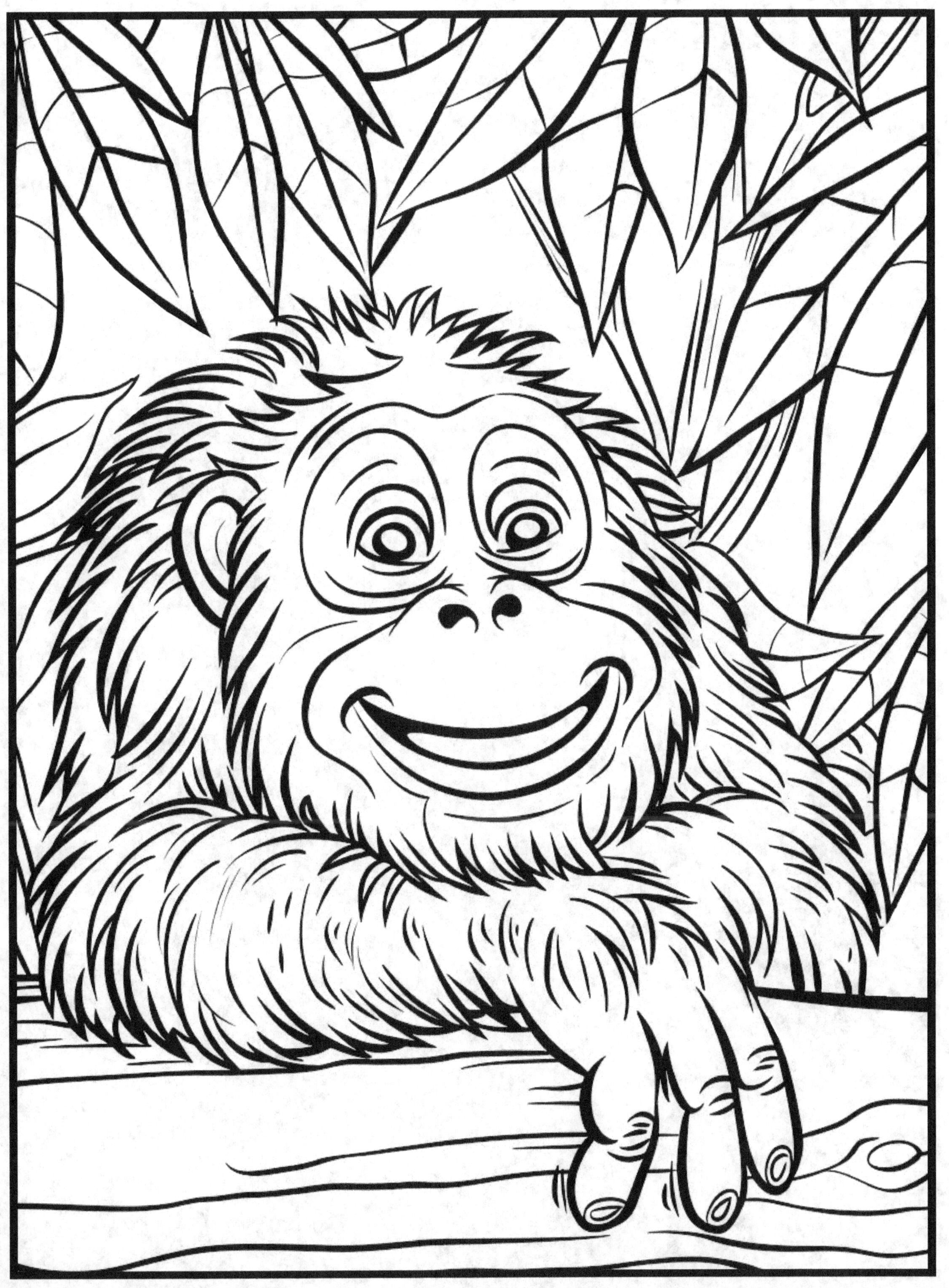

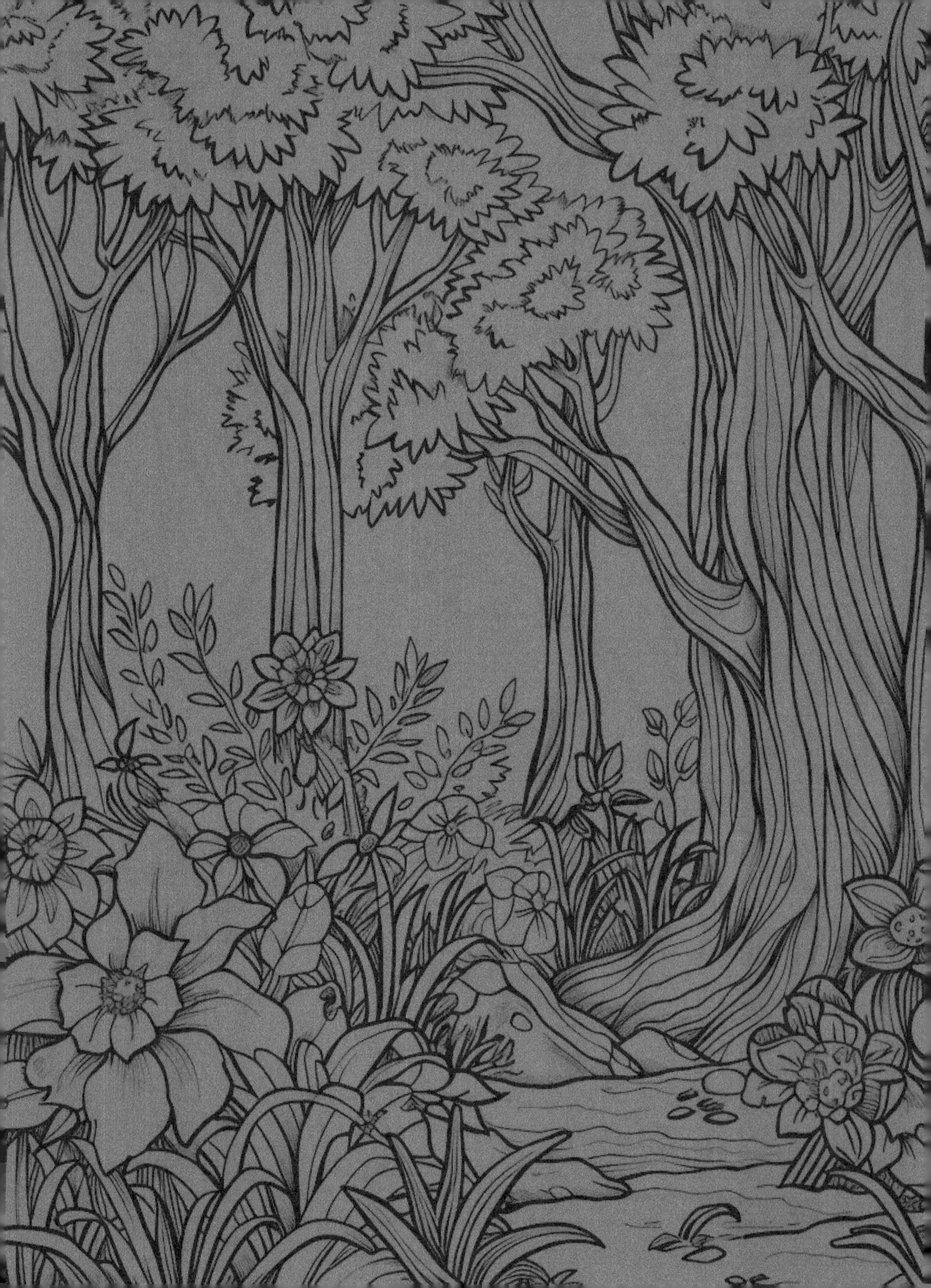

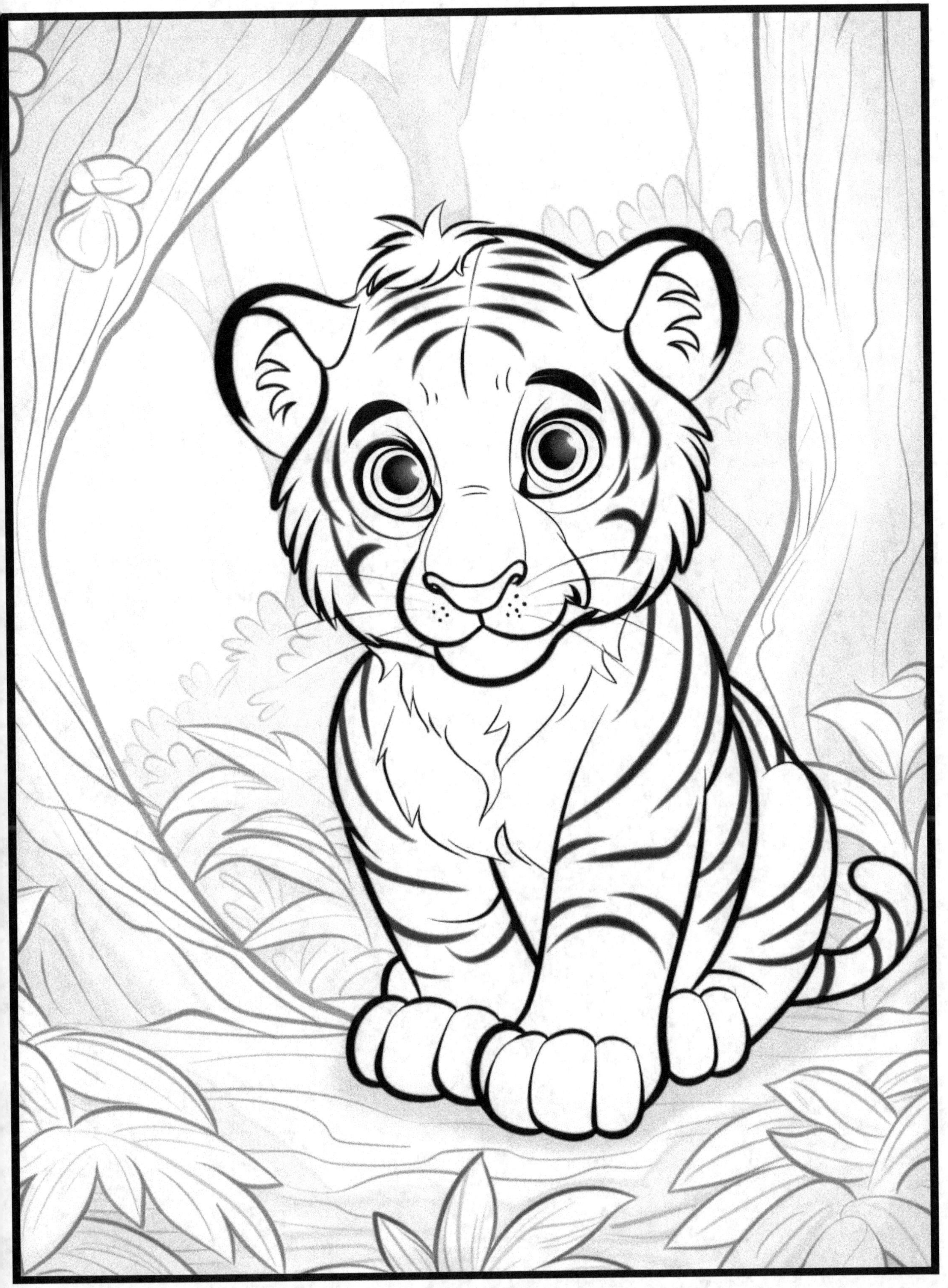

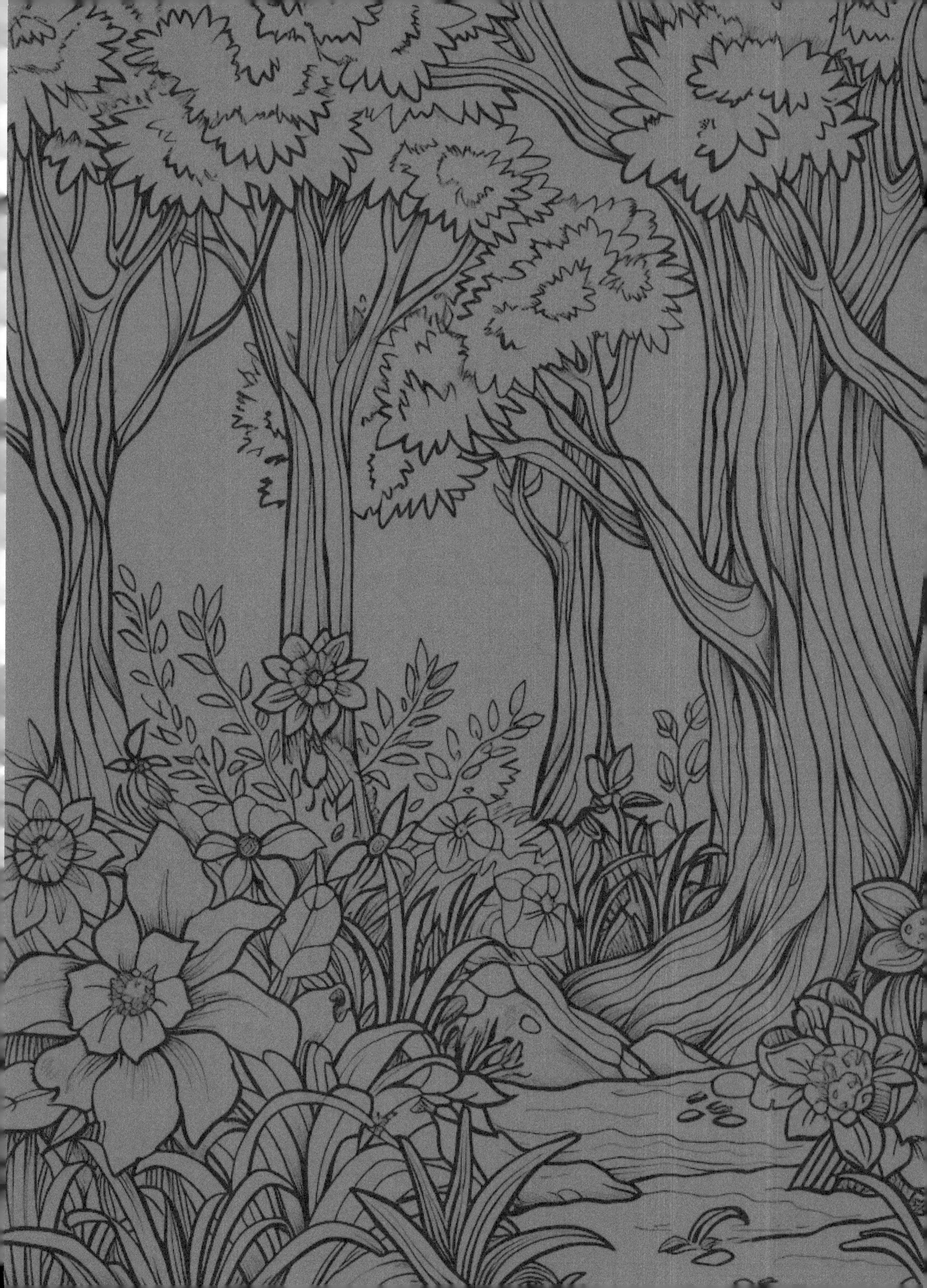

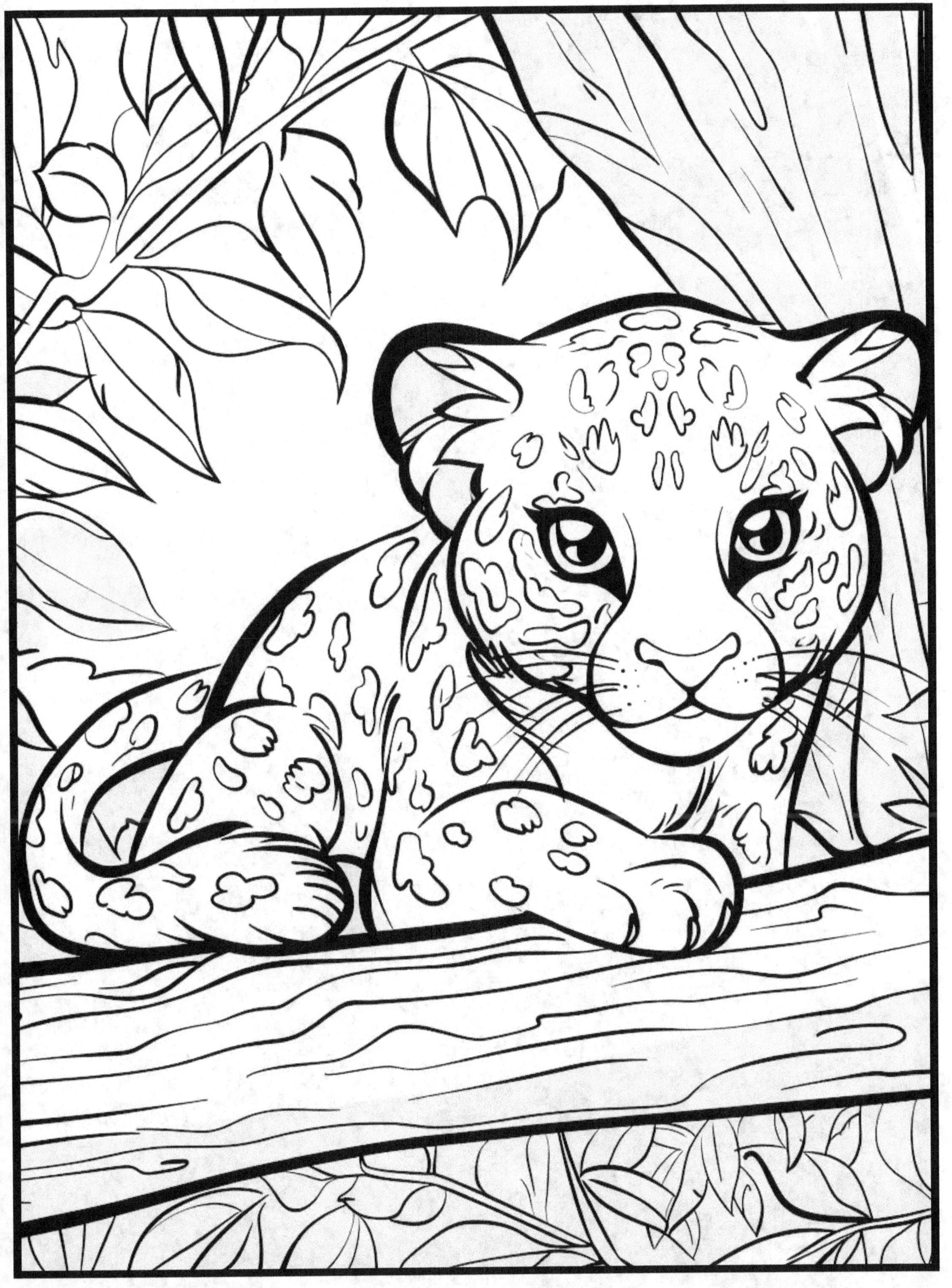

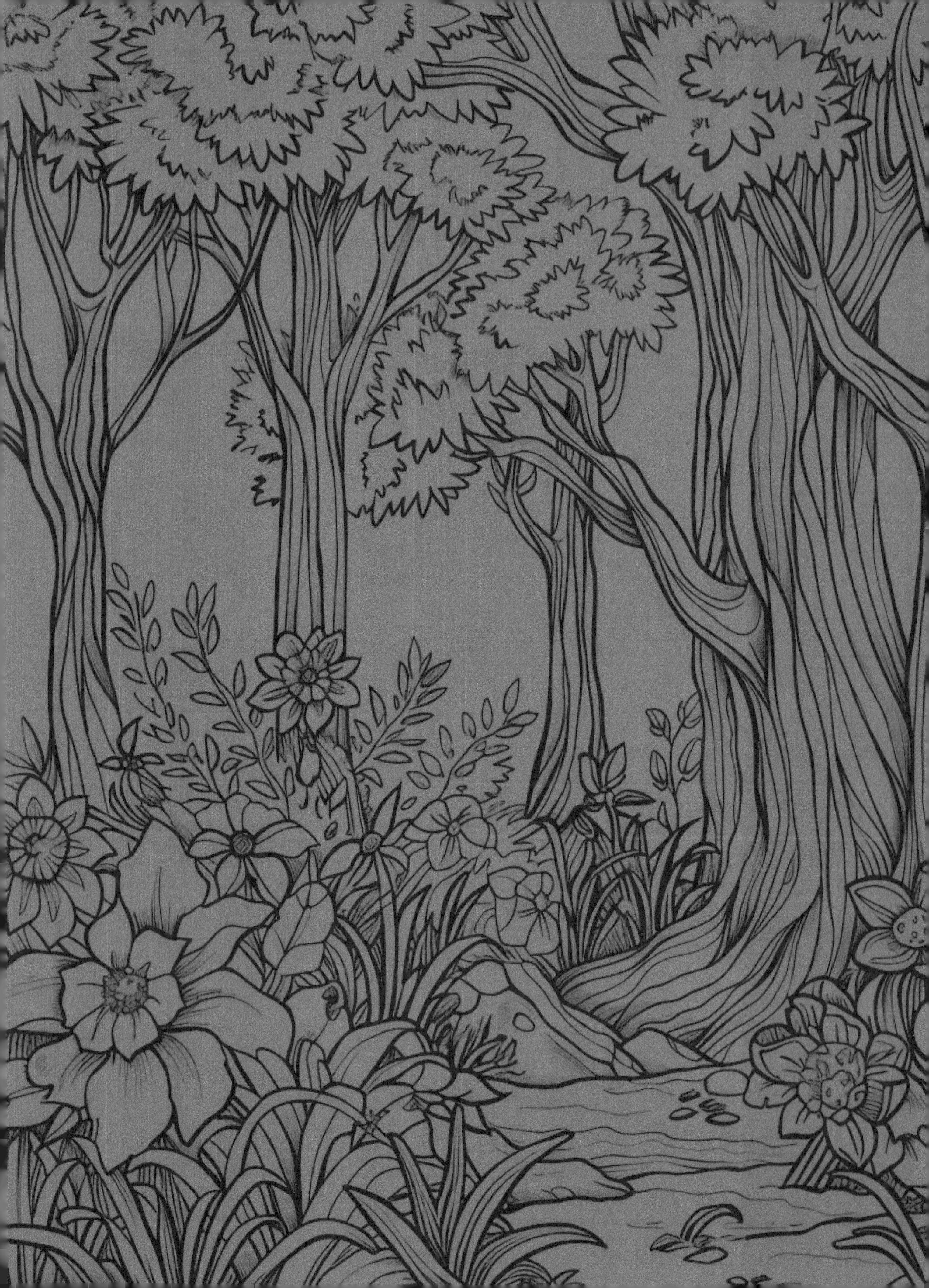

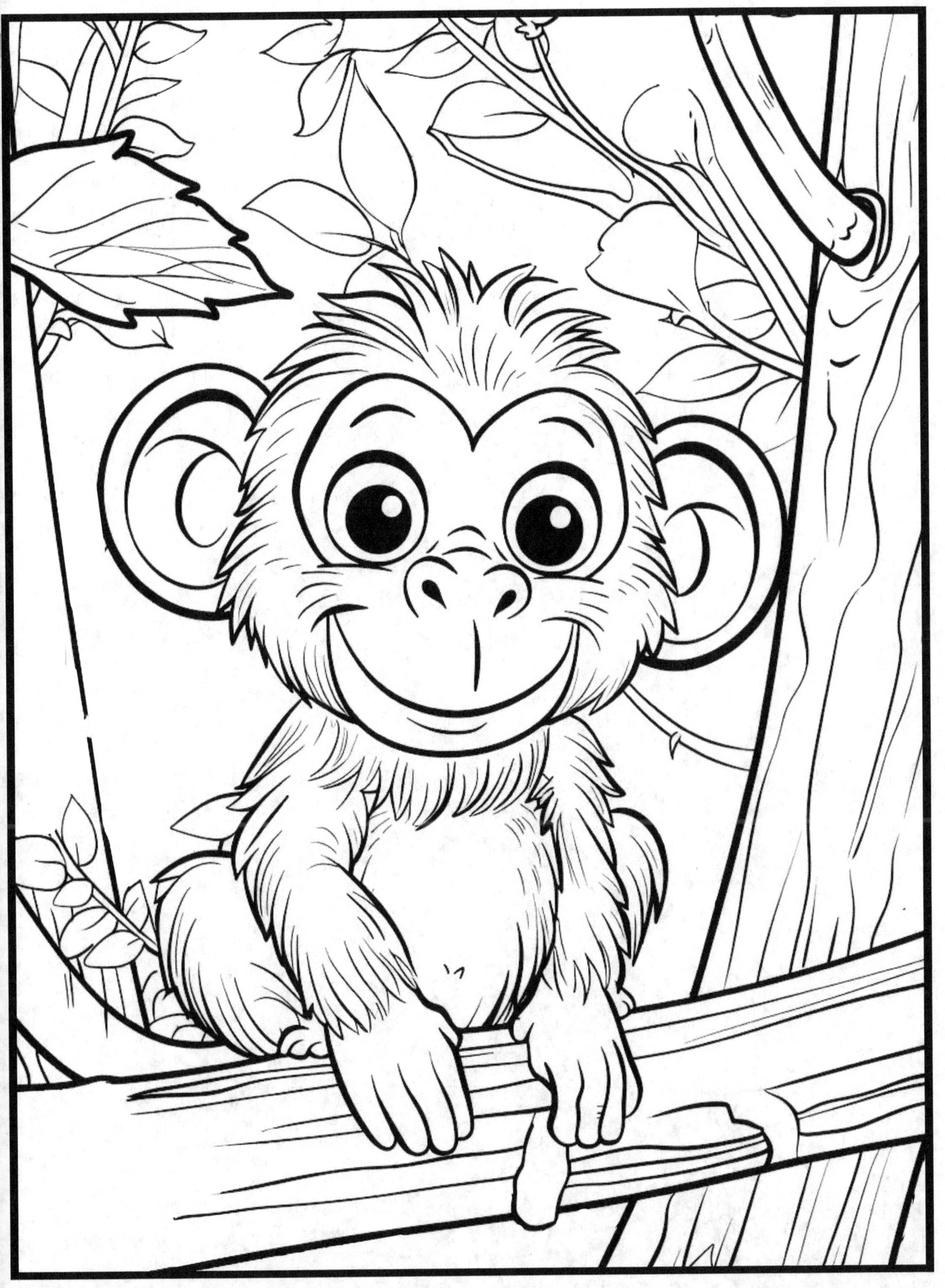

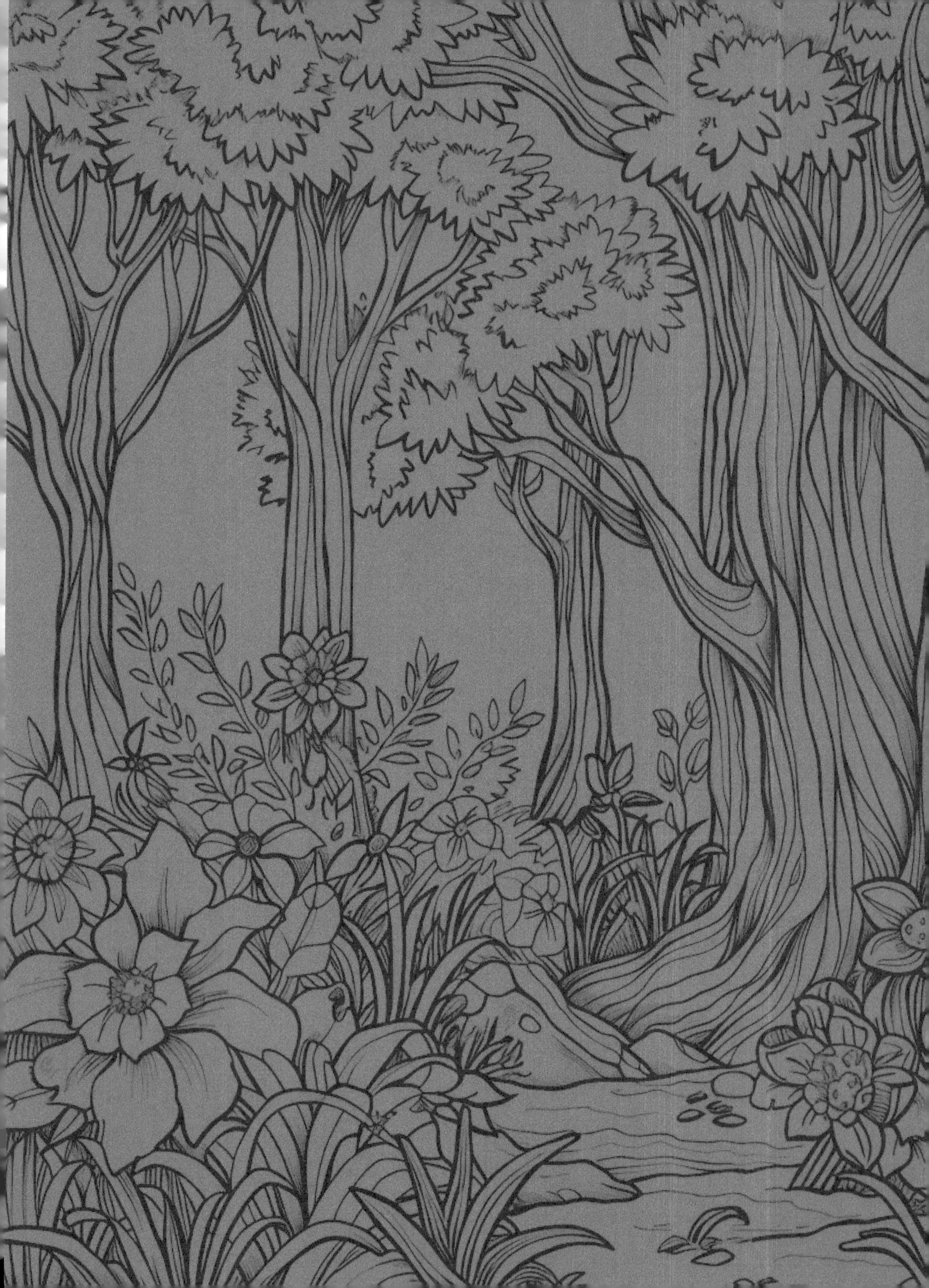

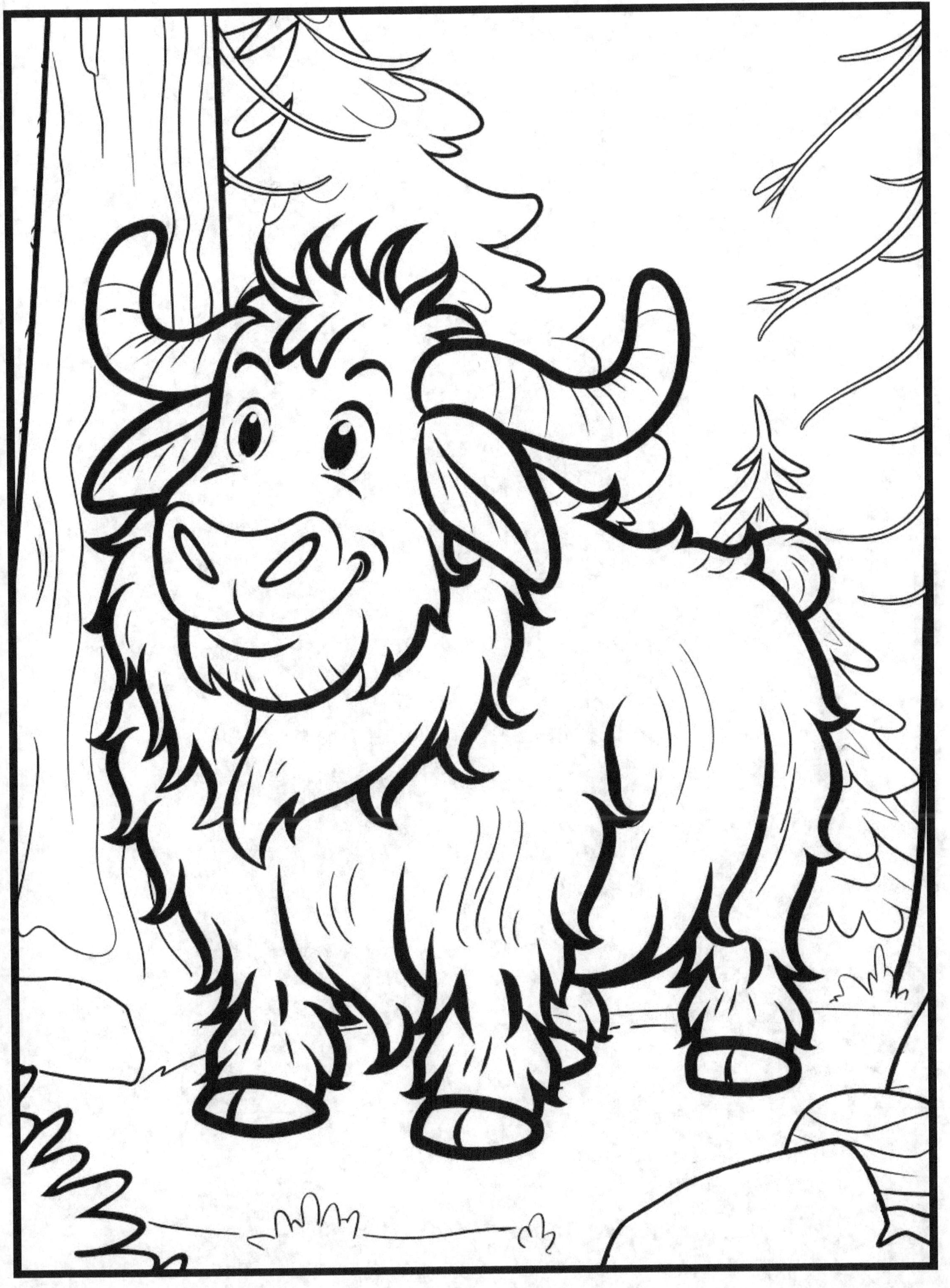

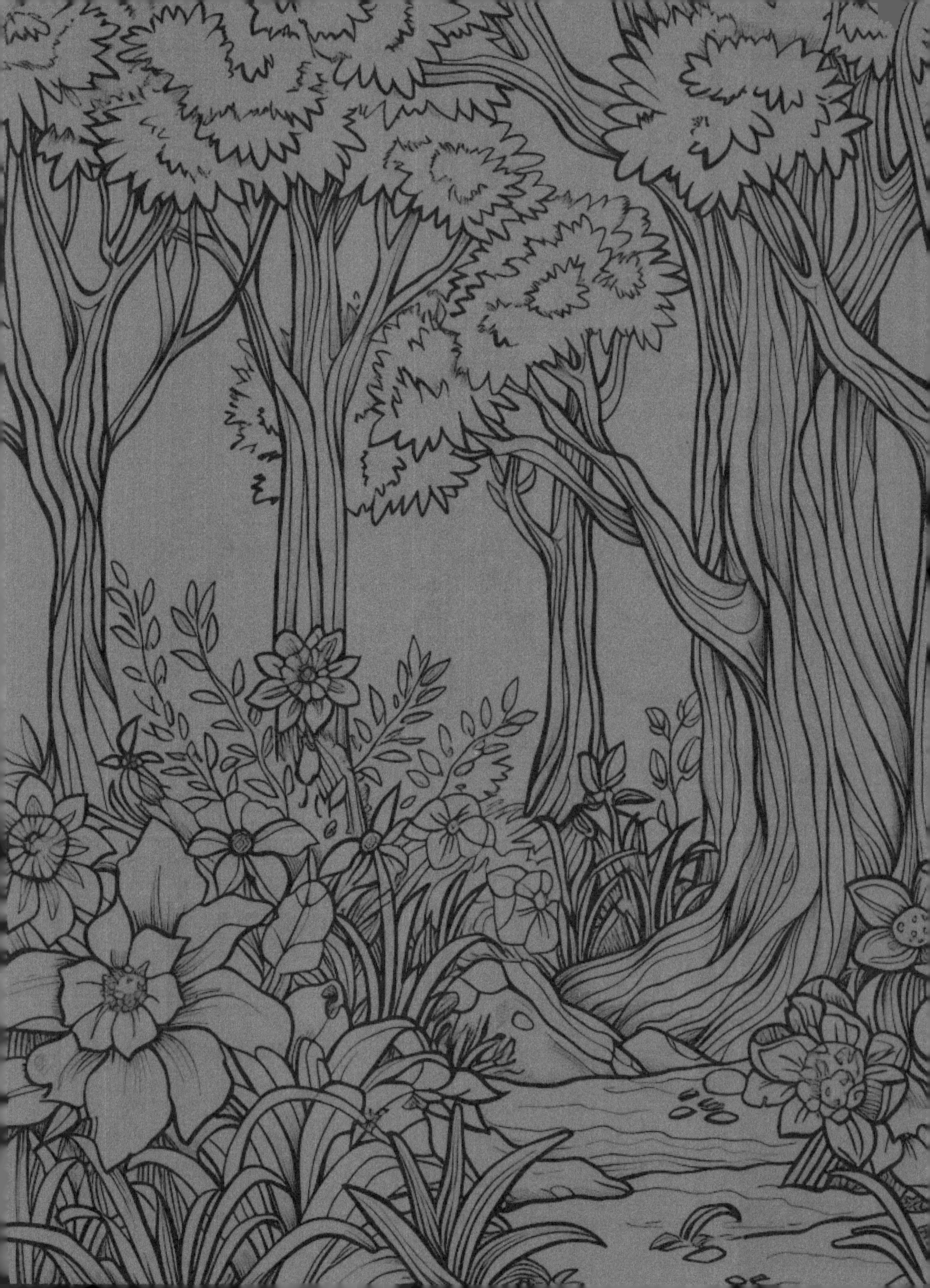

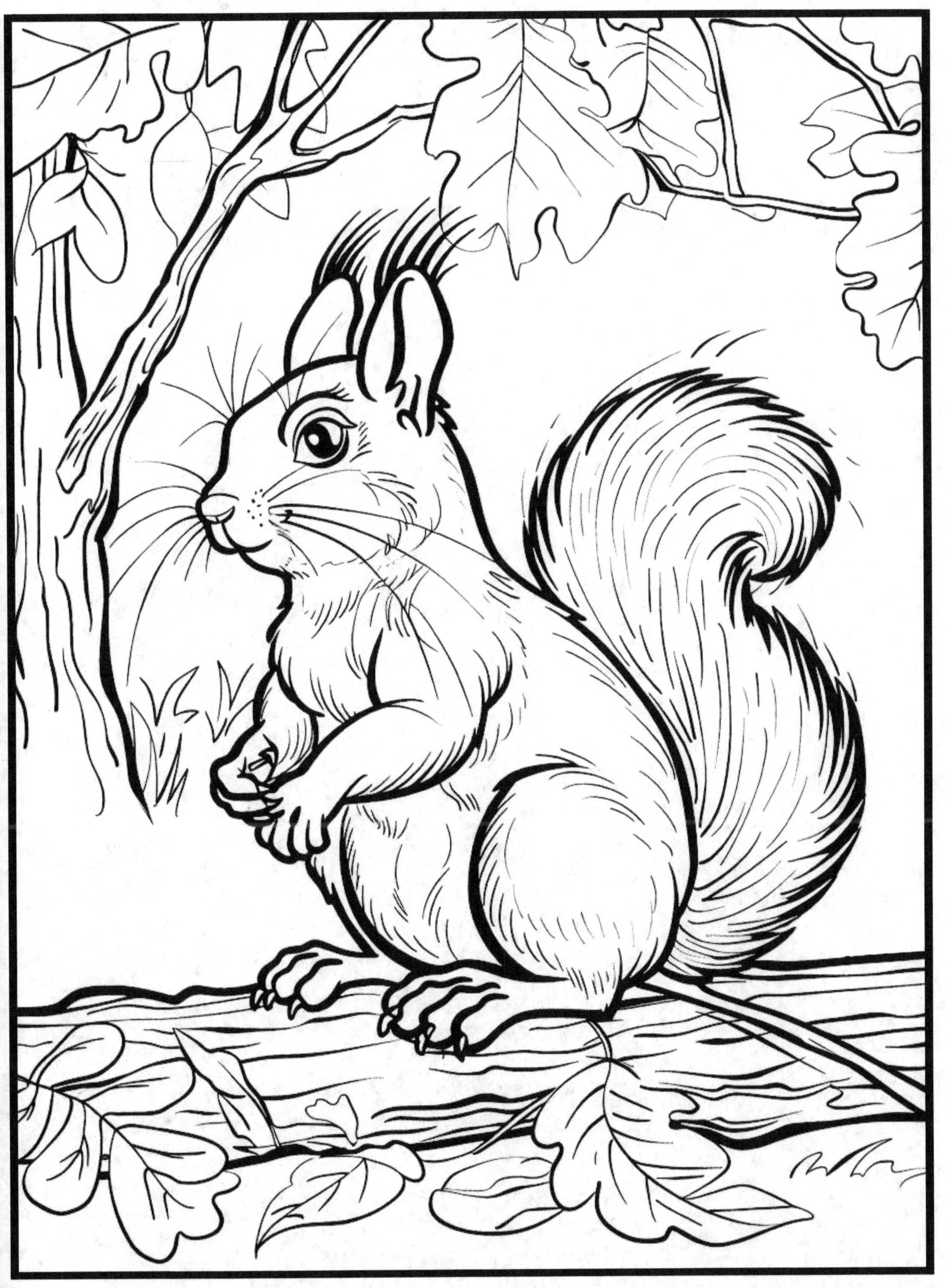

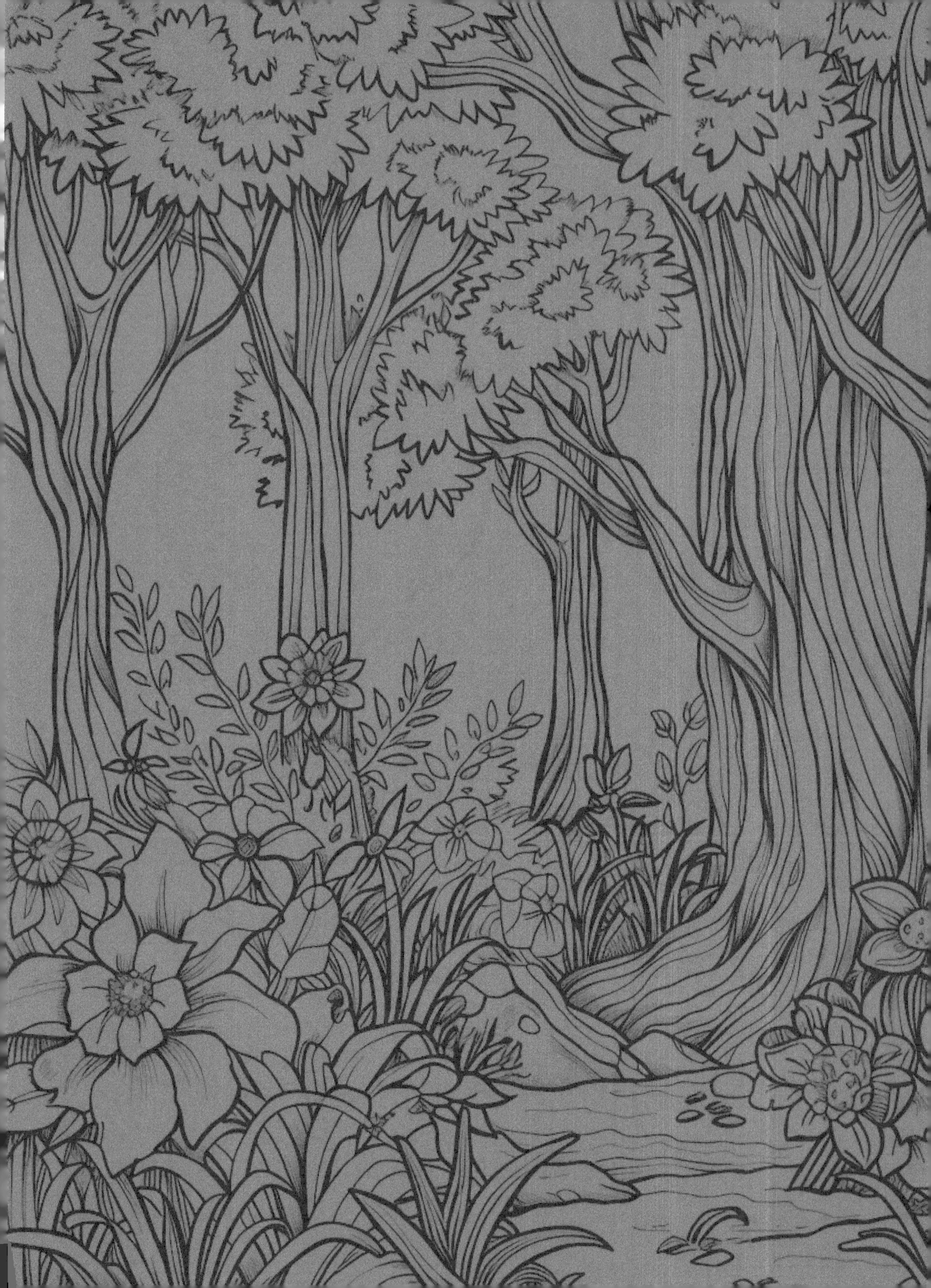

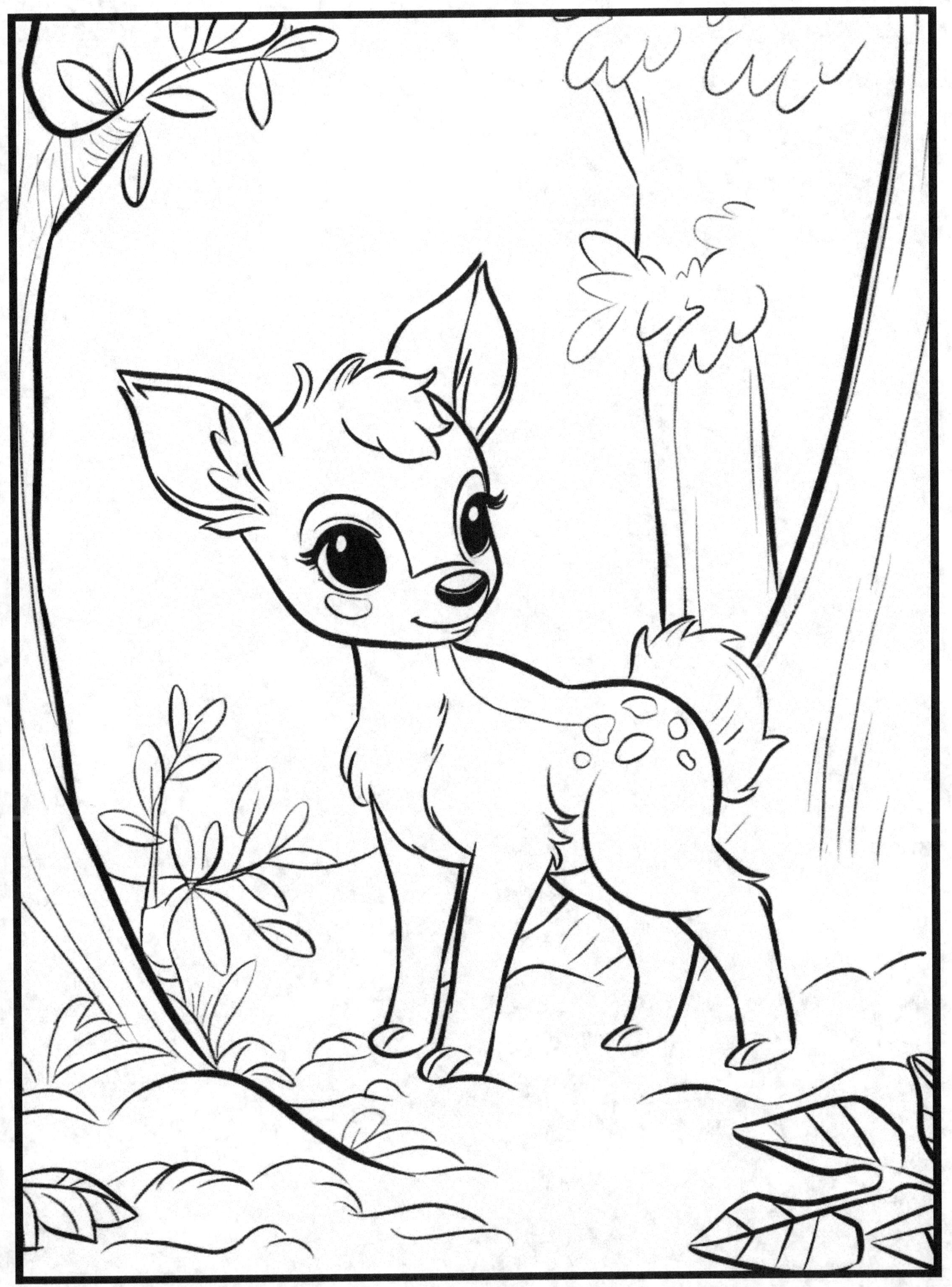

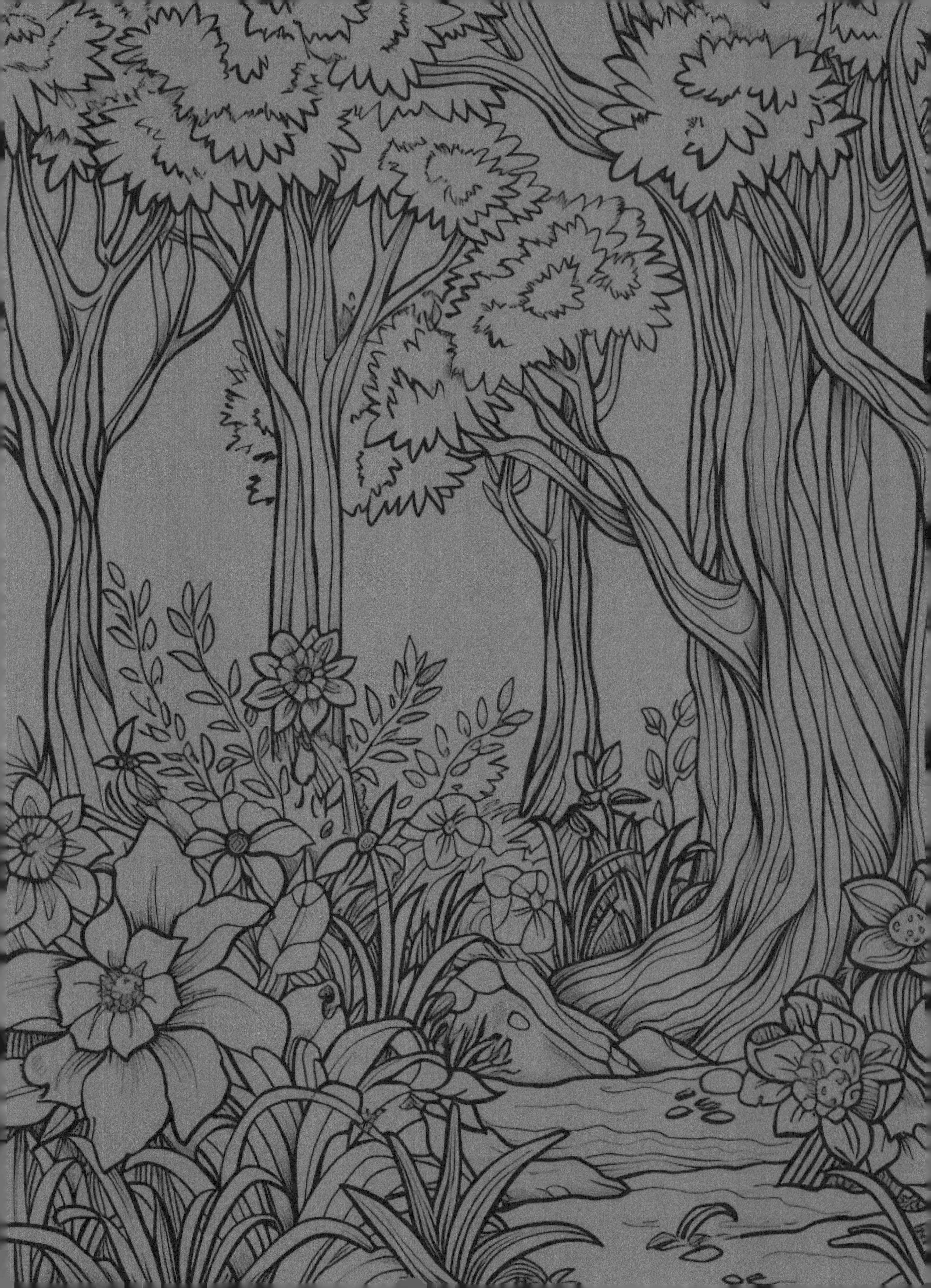

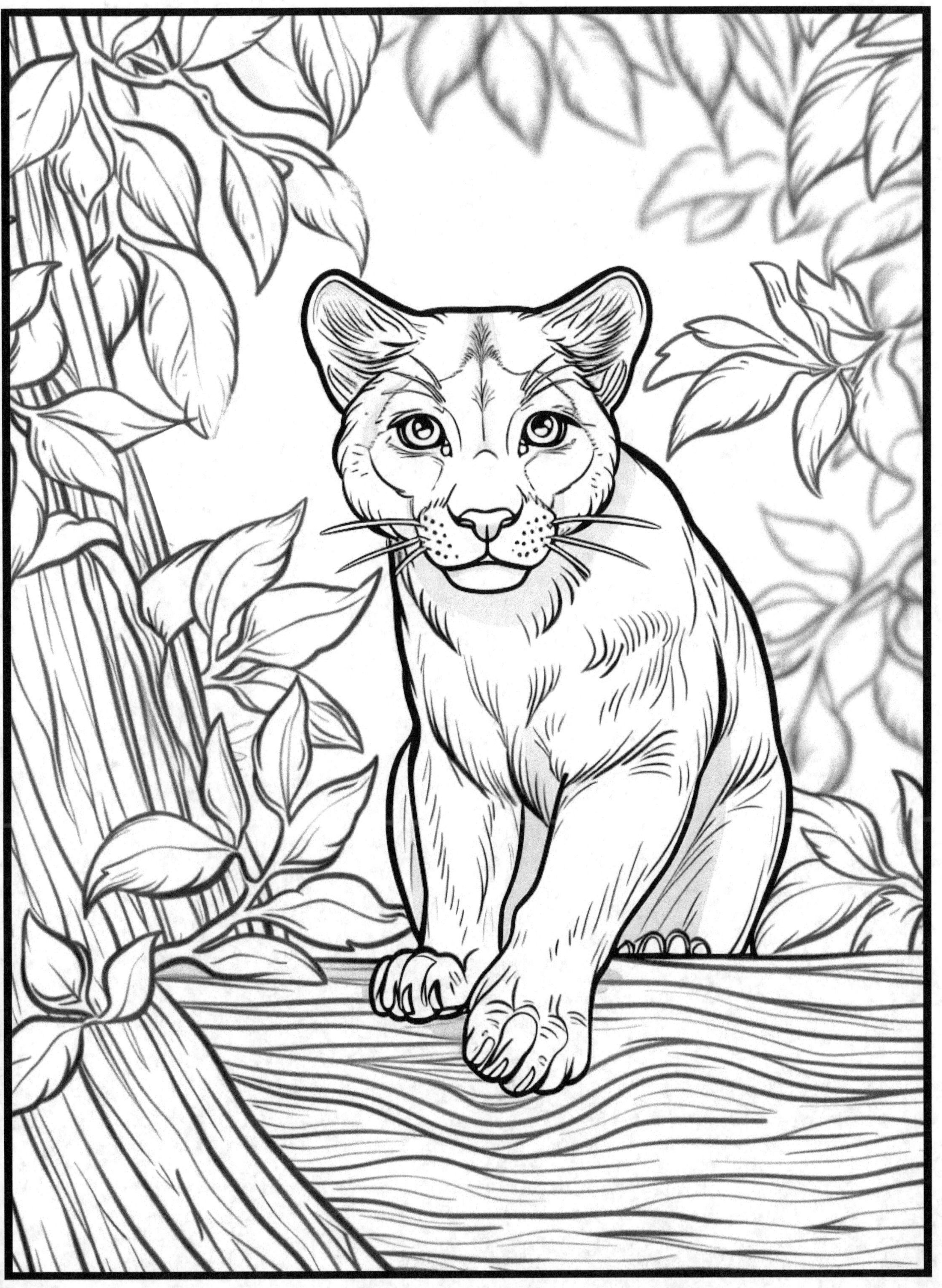

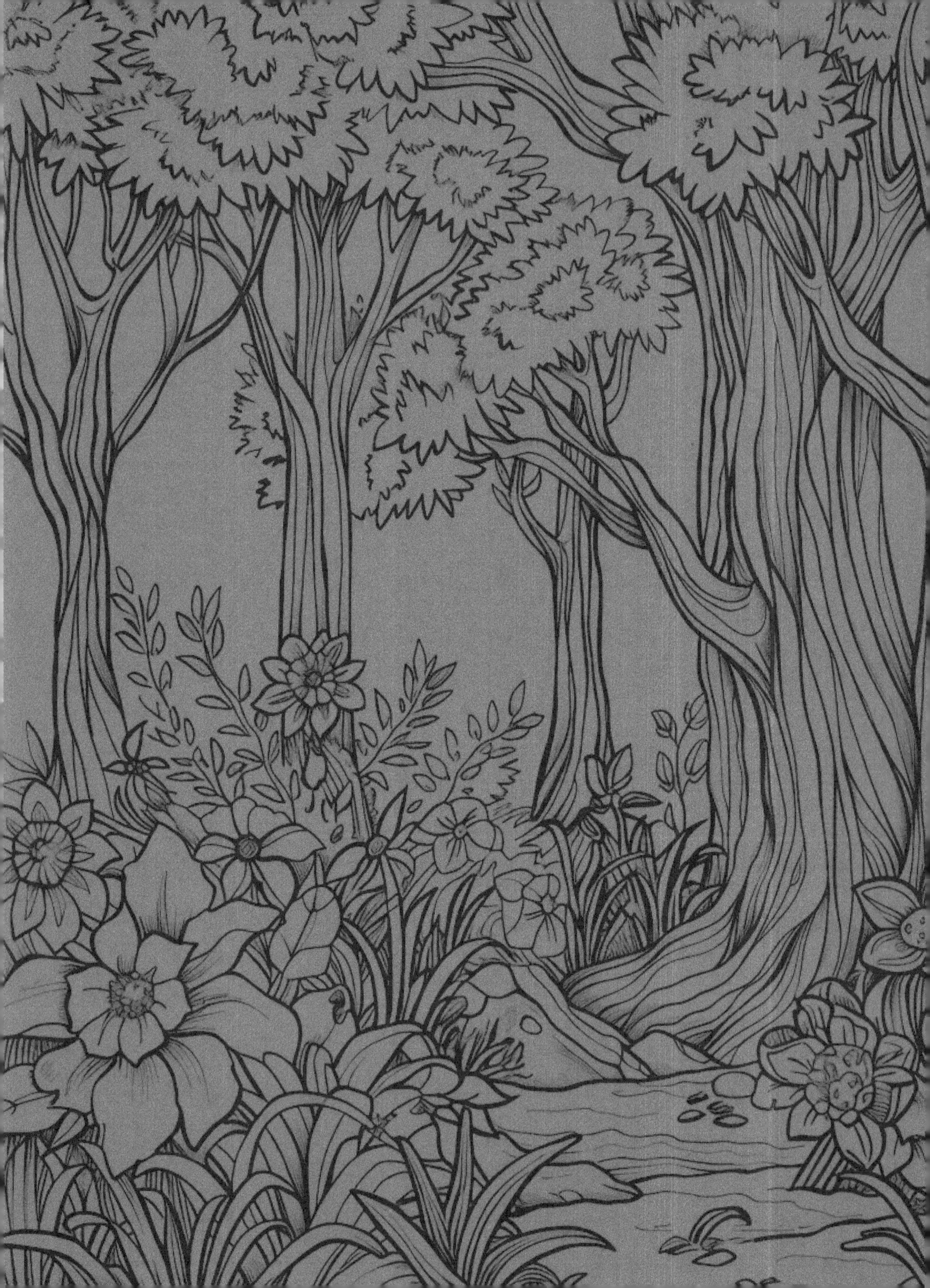

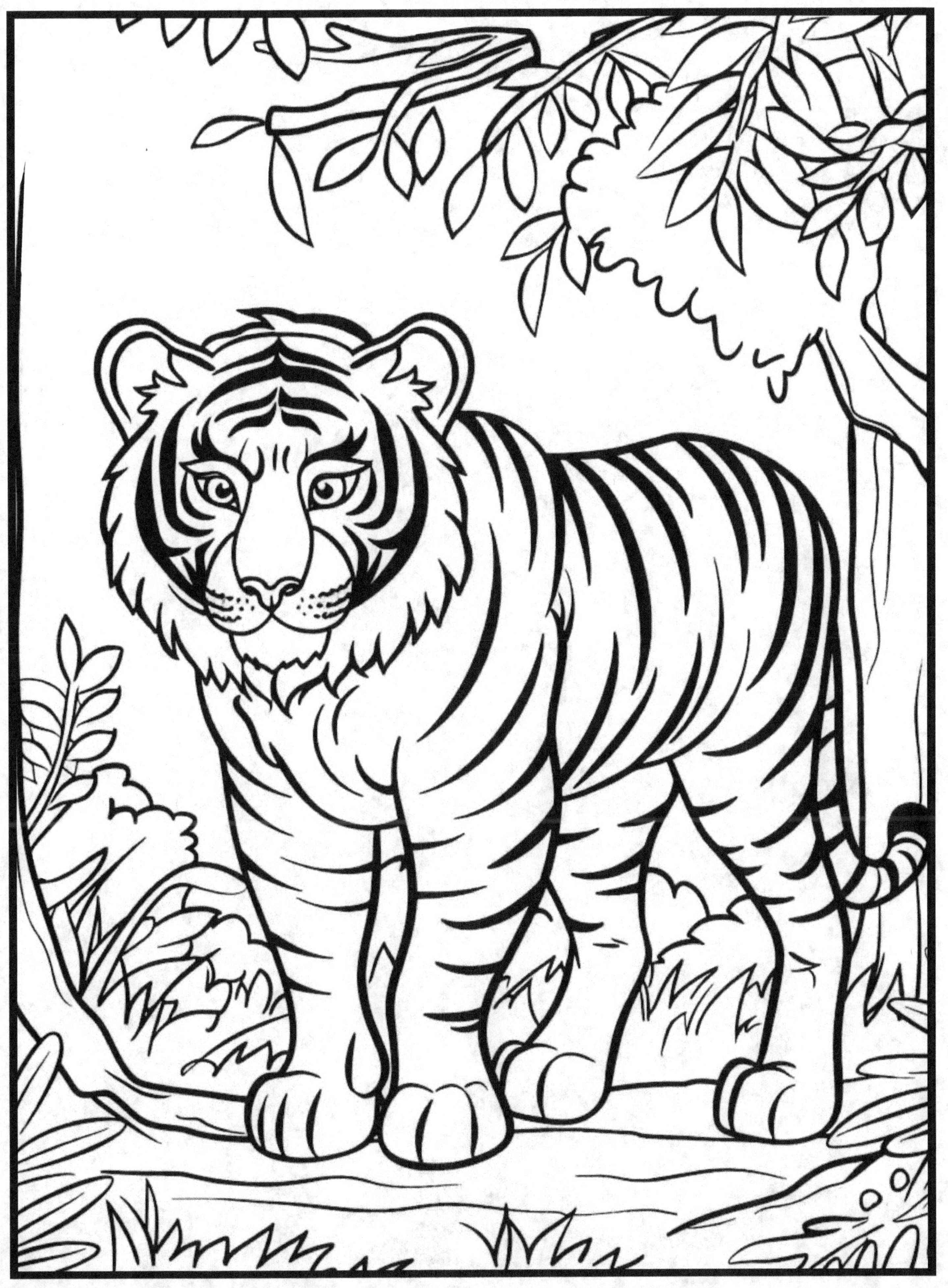

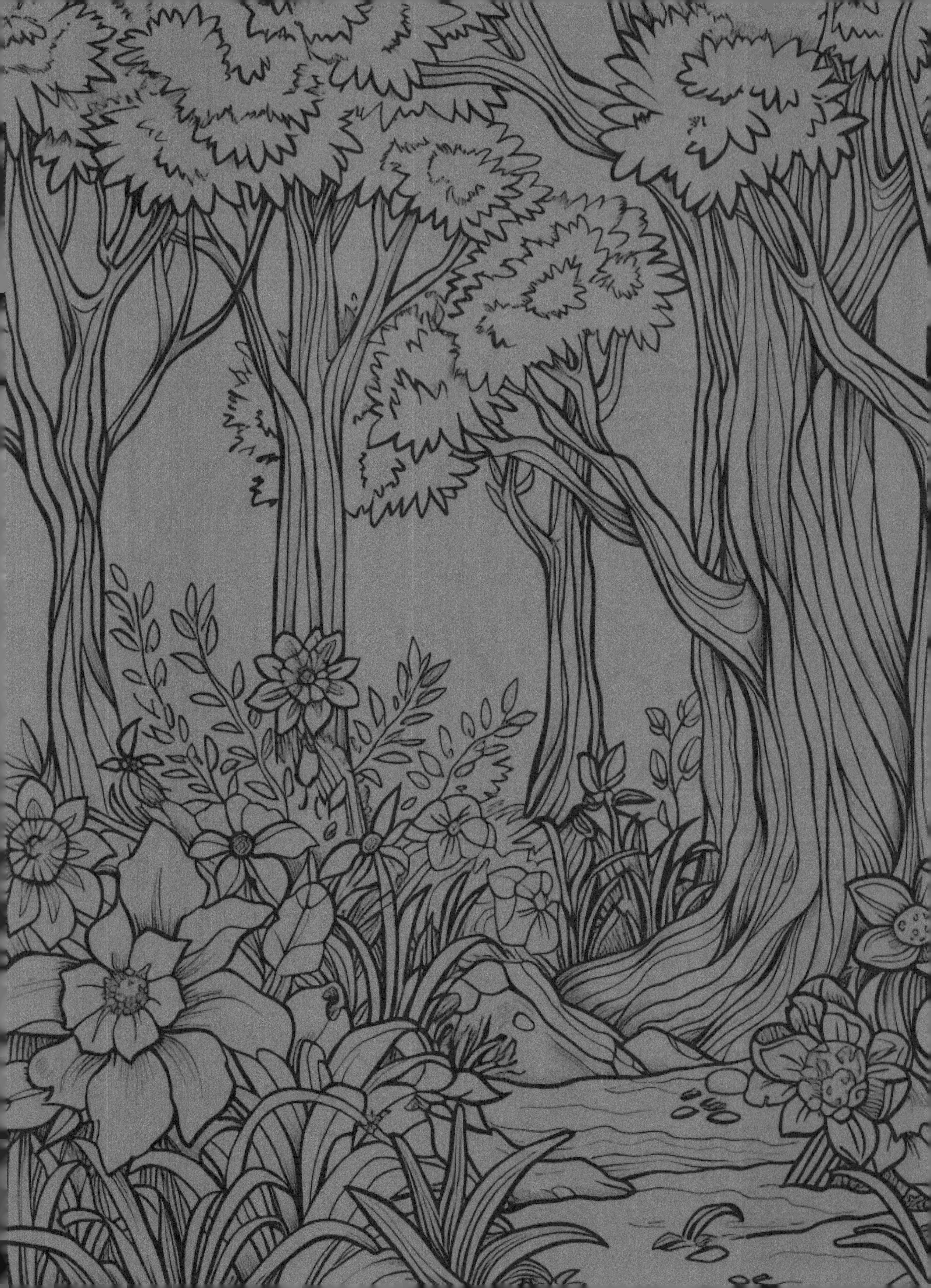

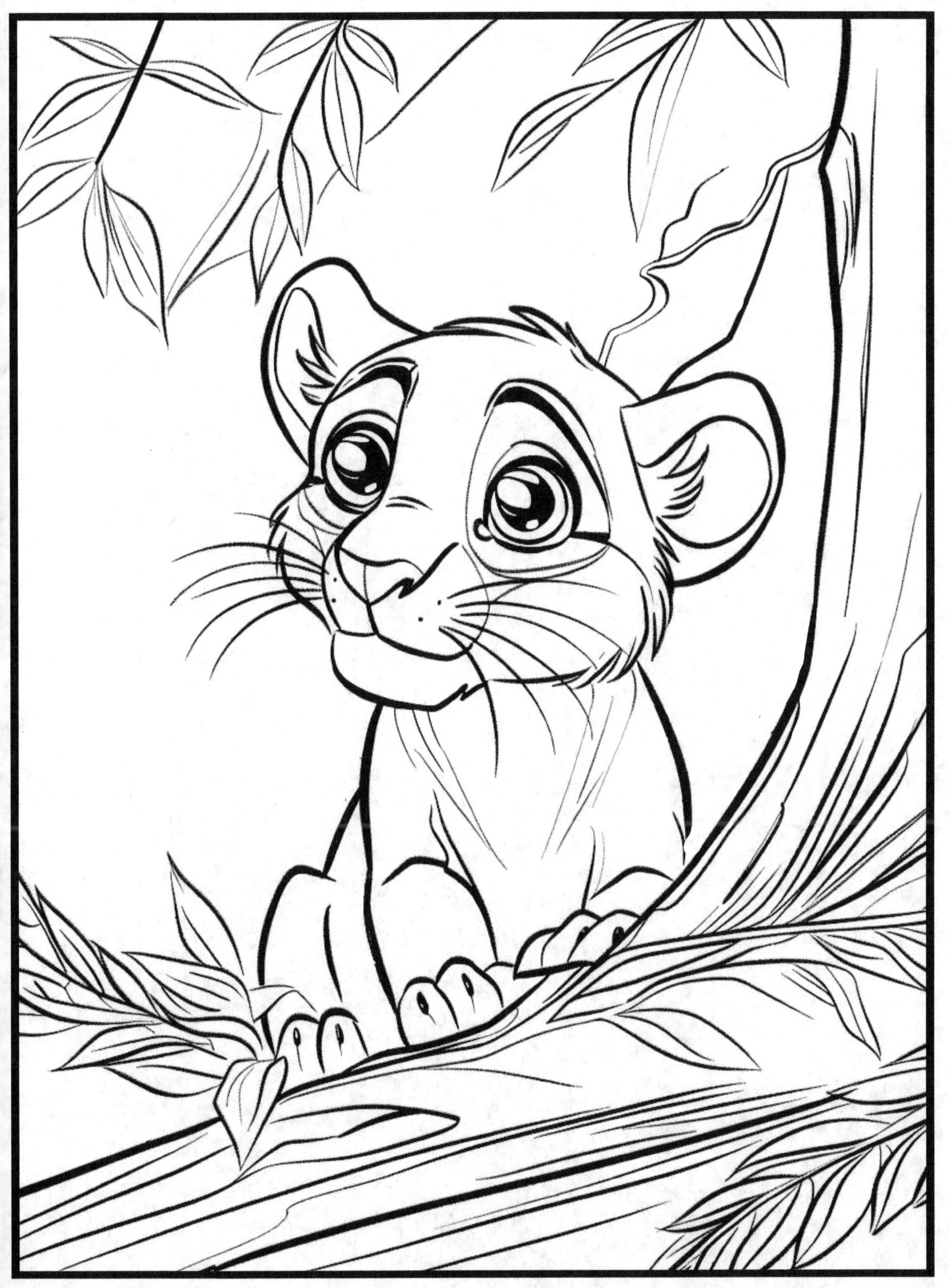

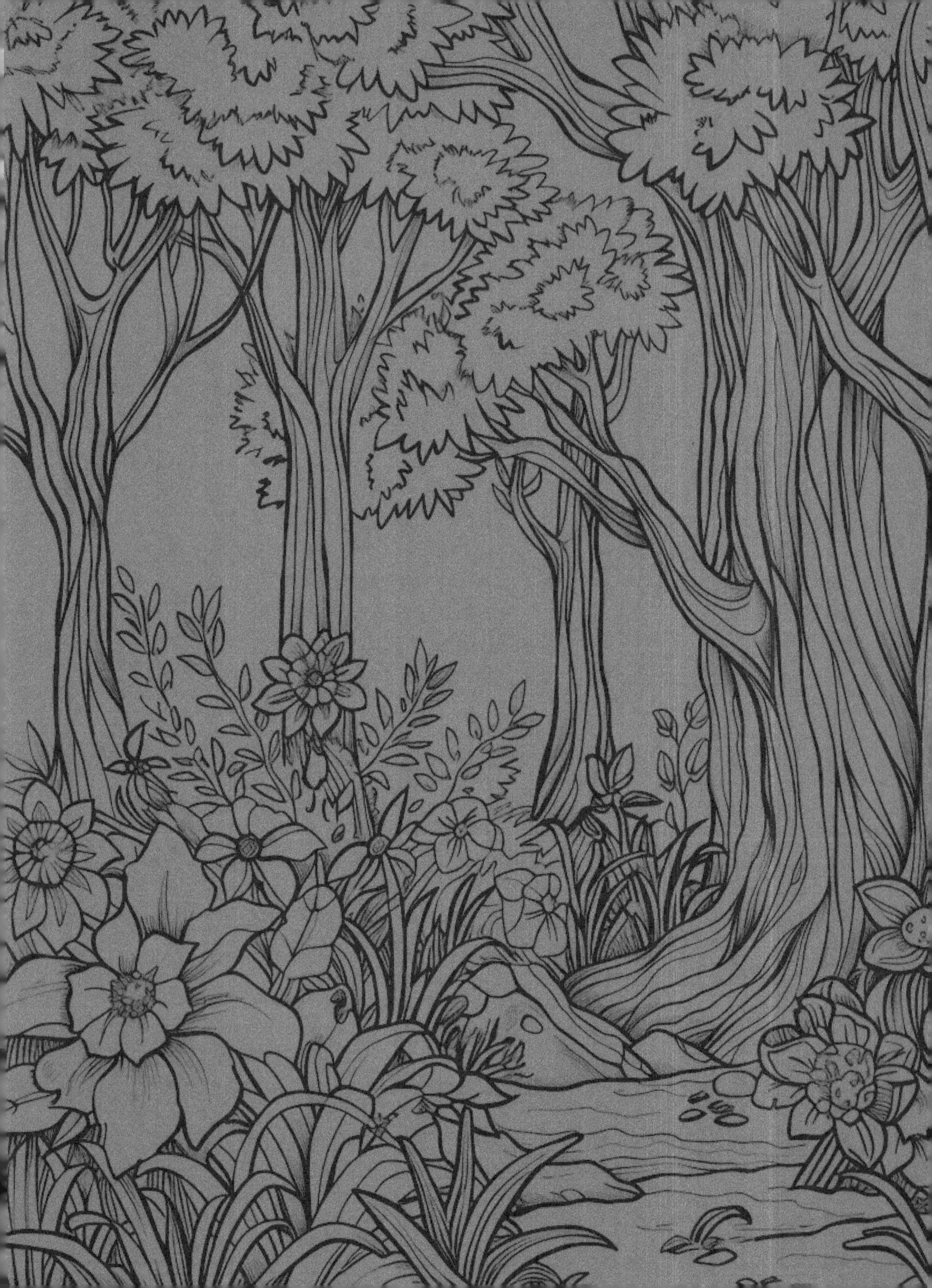

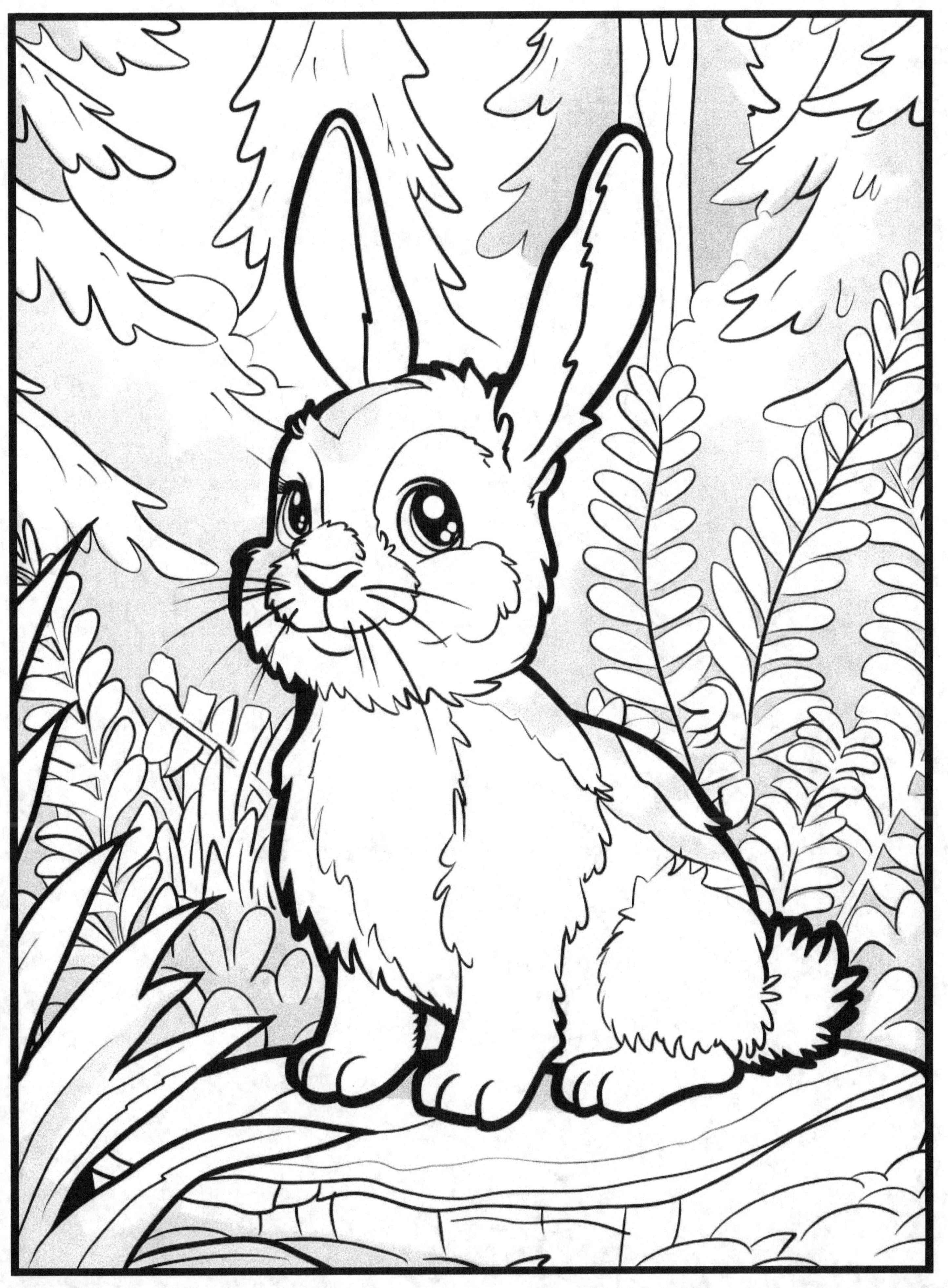

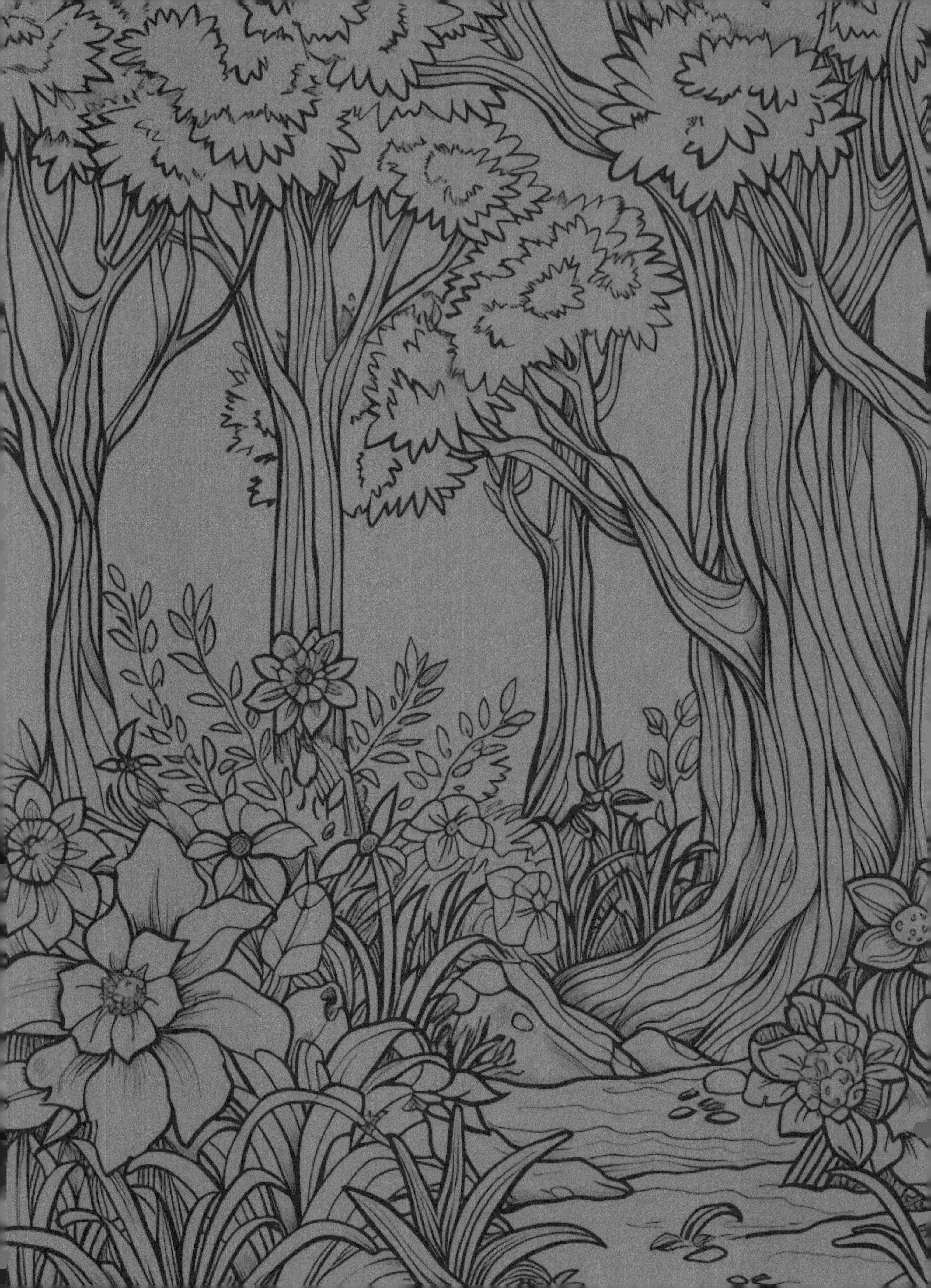

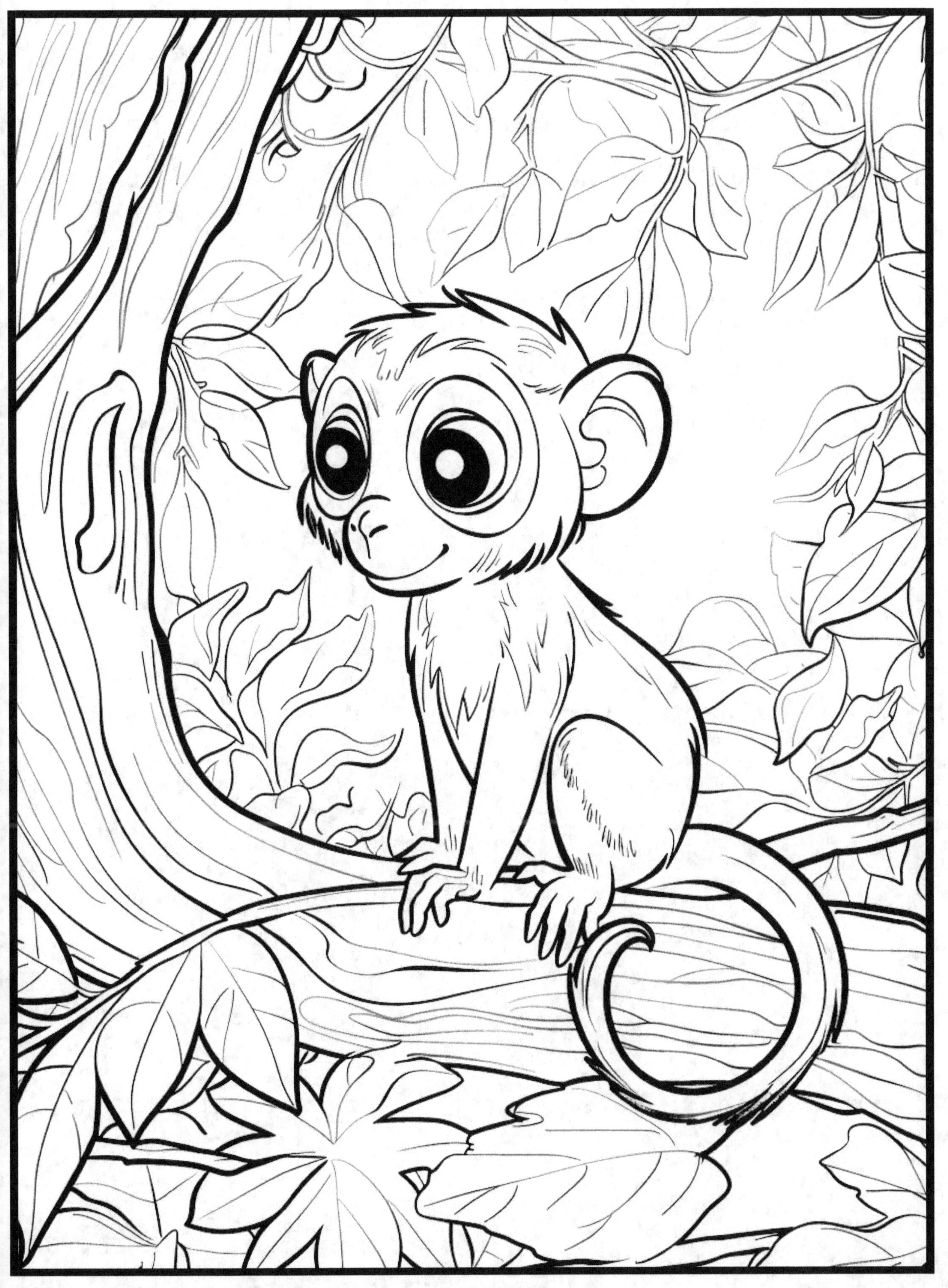

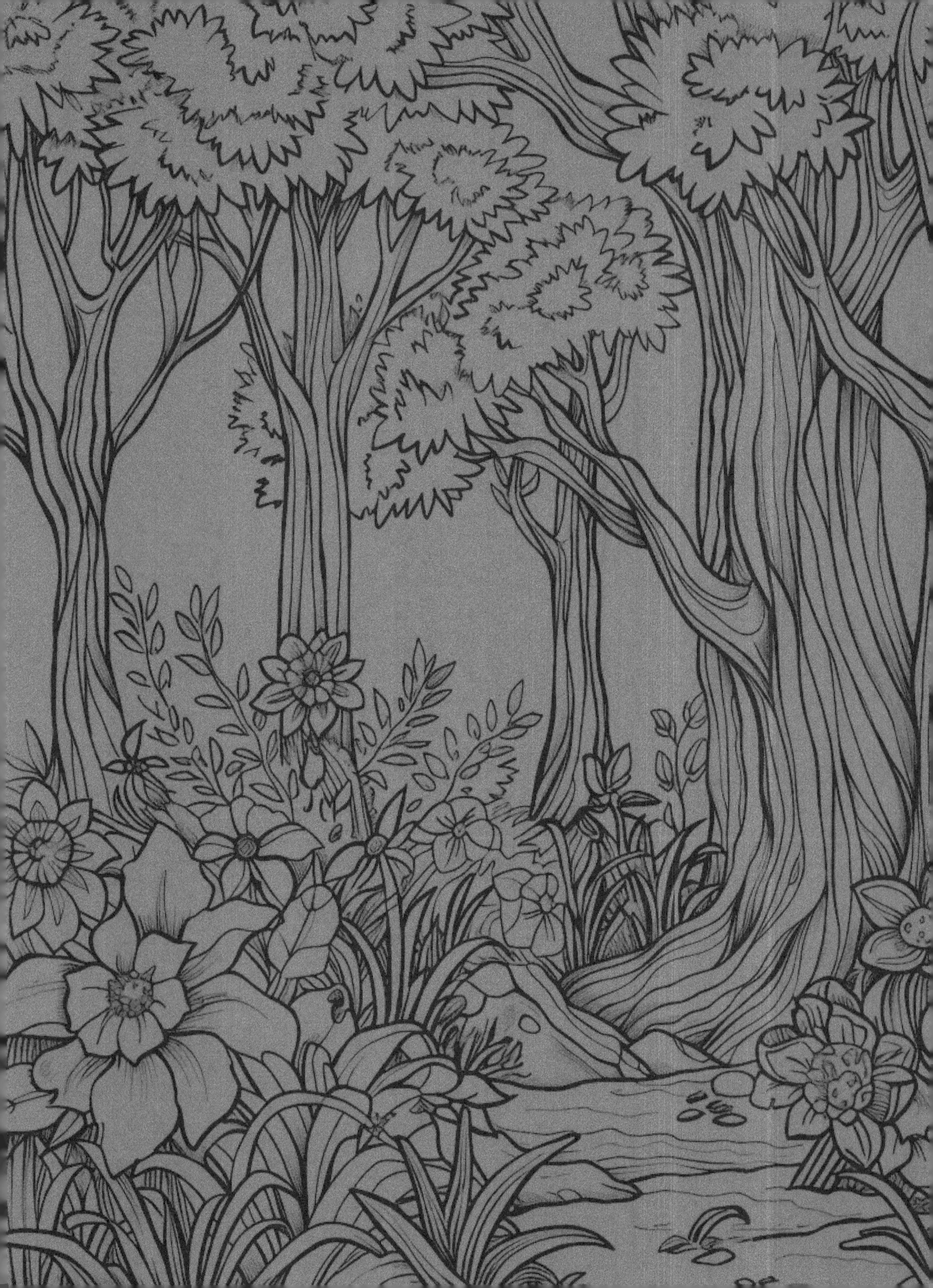

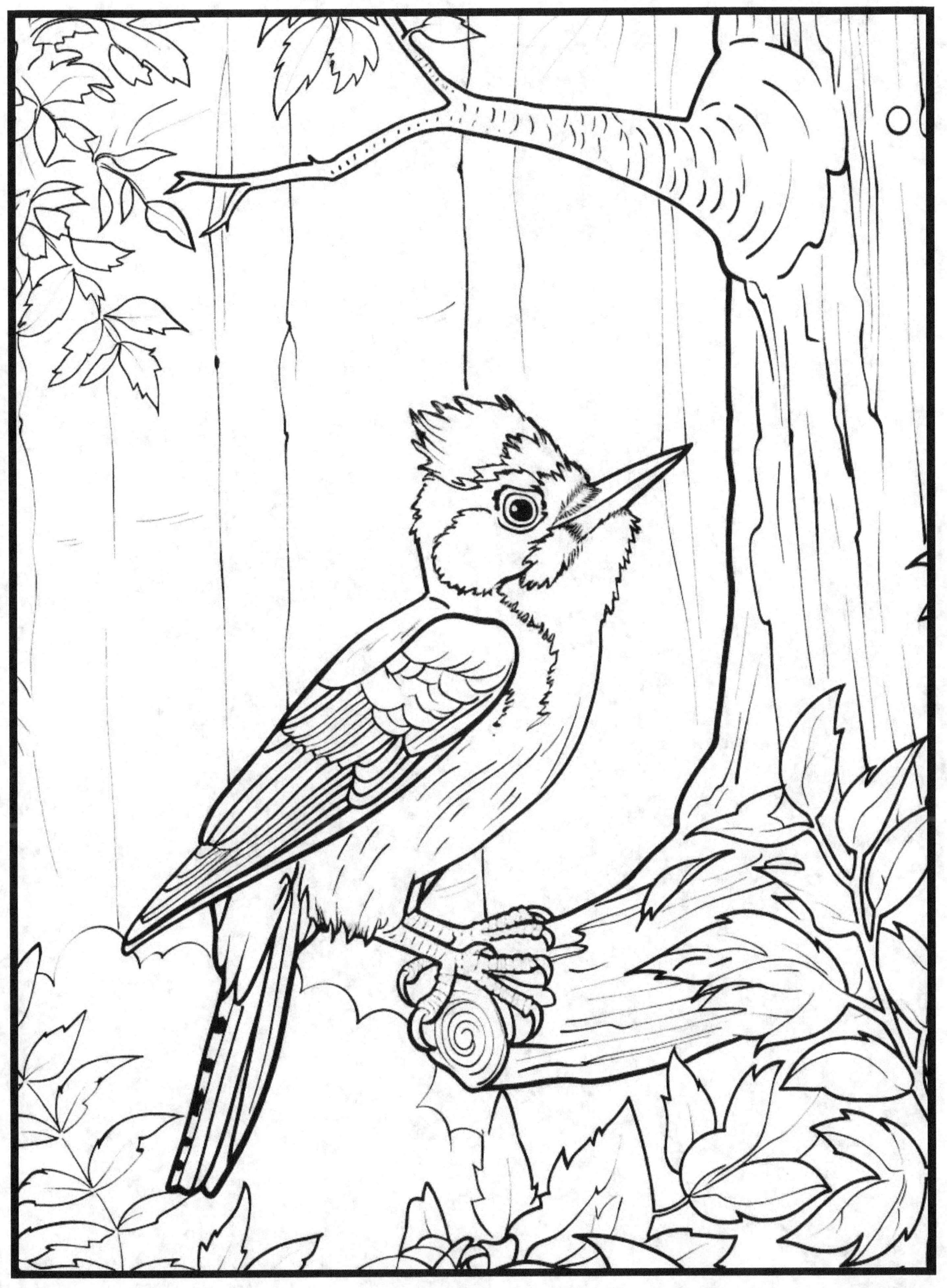

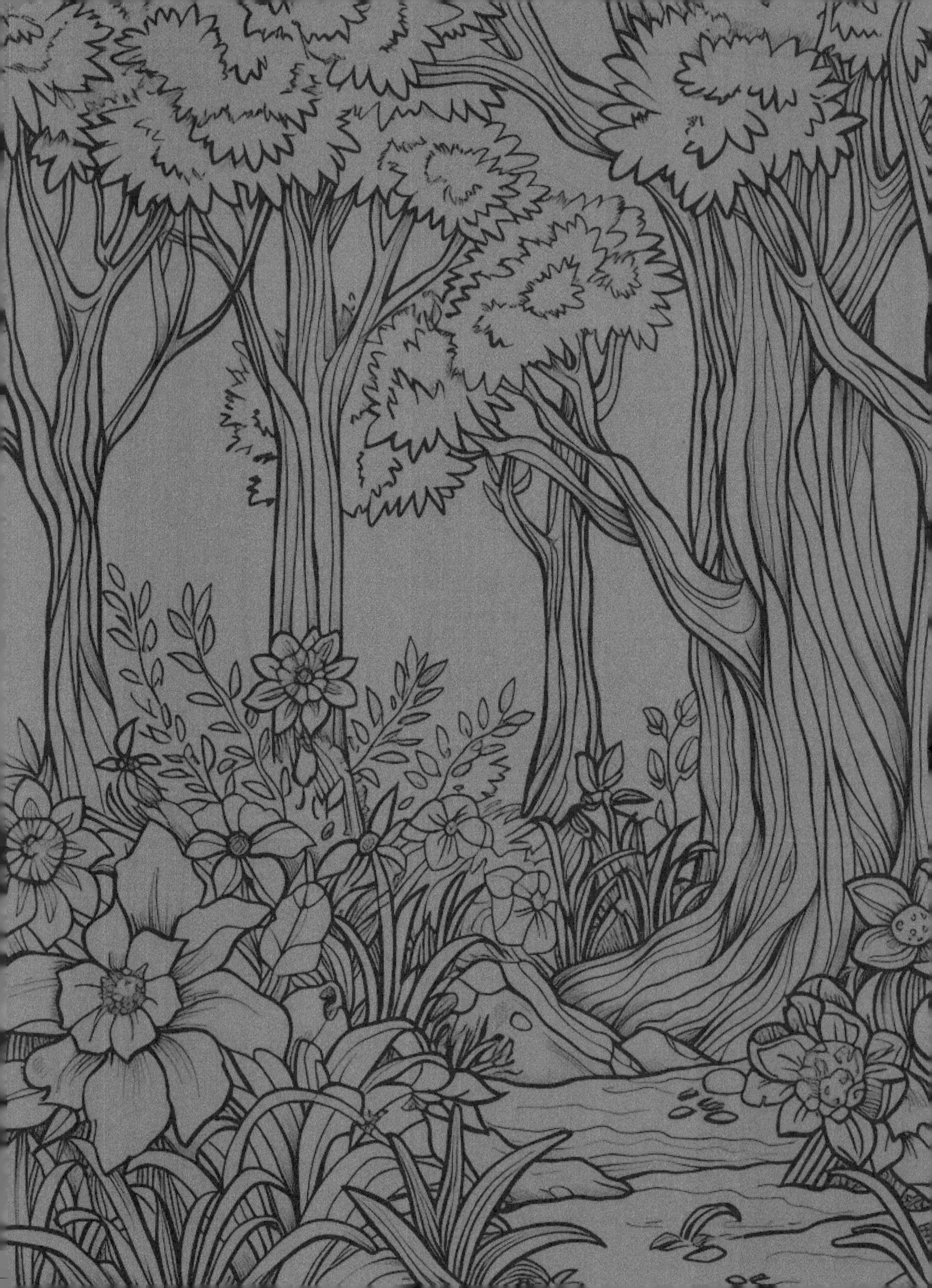

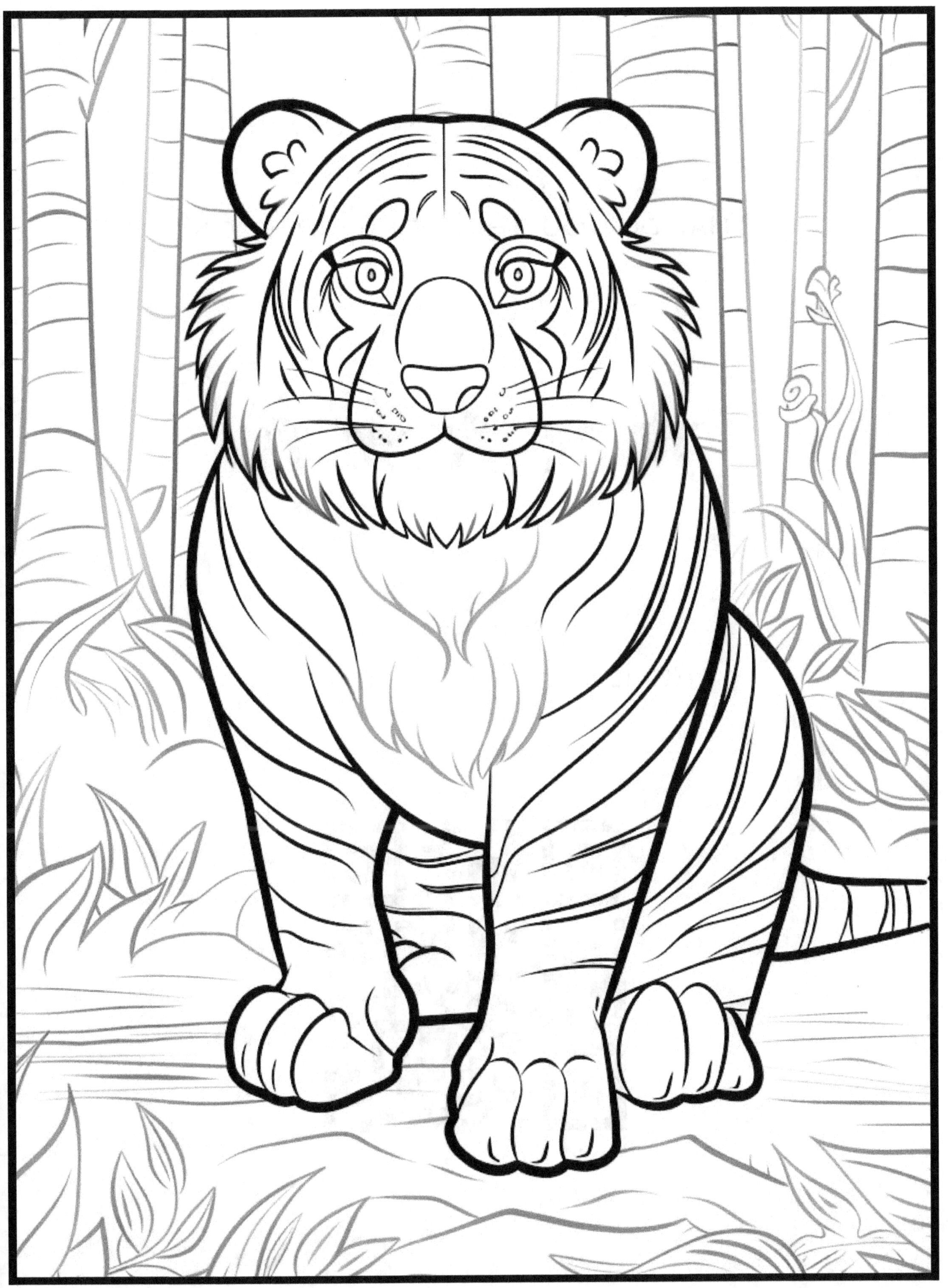

What do you think of our book?

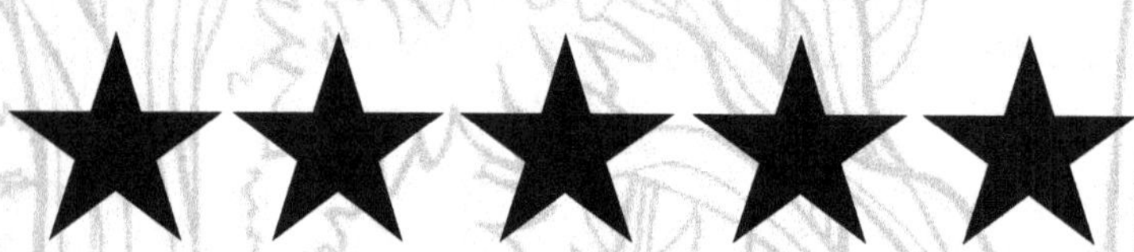

Please!!!
Review us for motivation

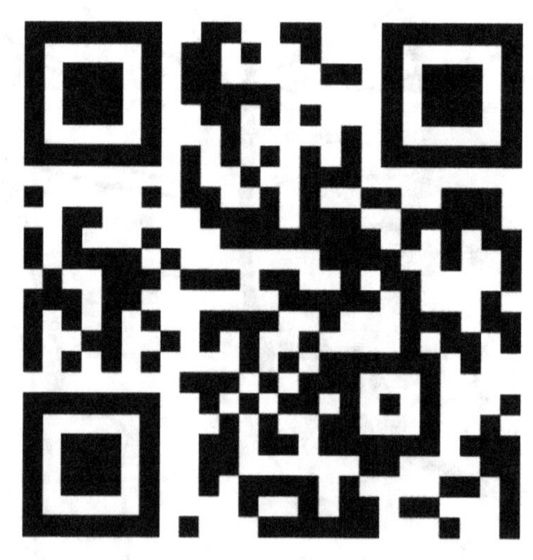

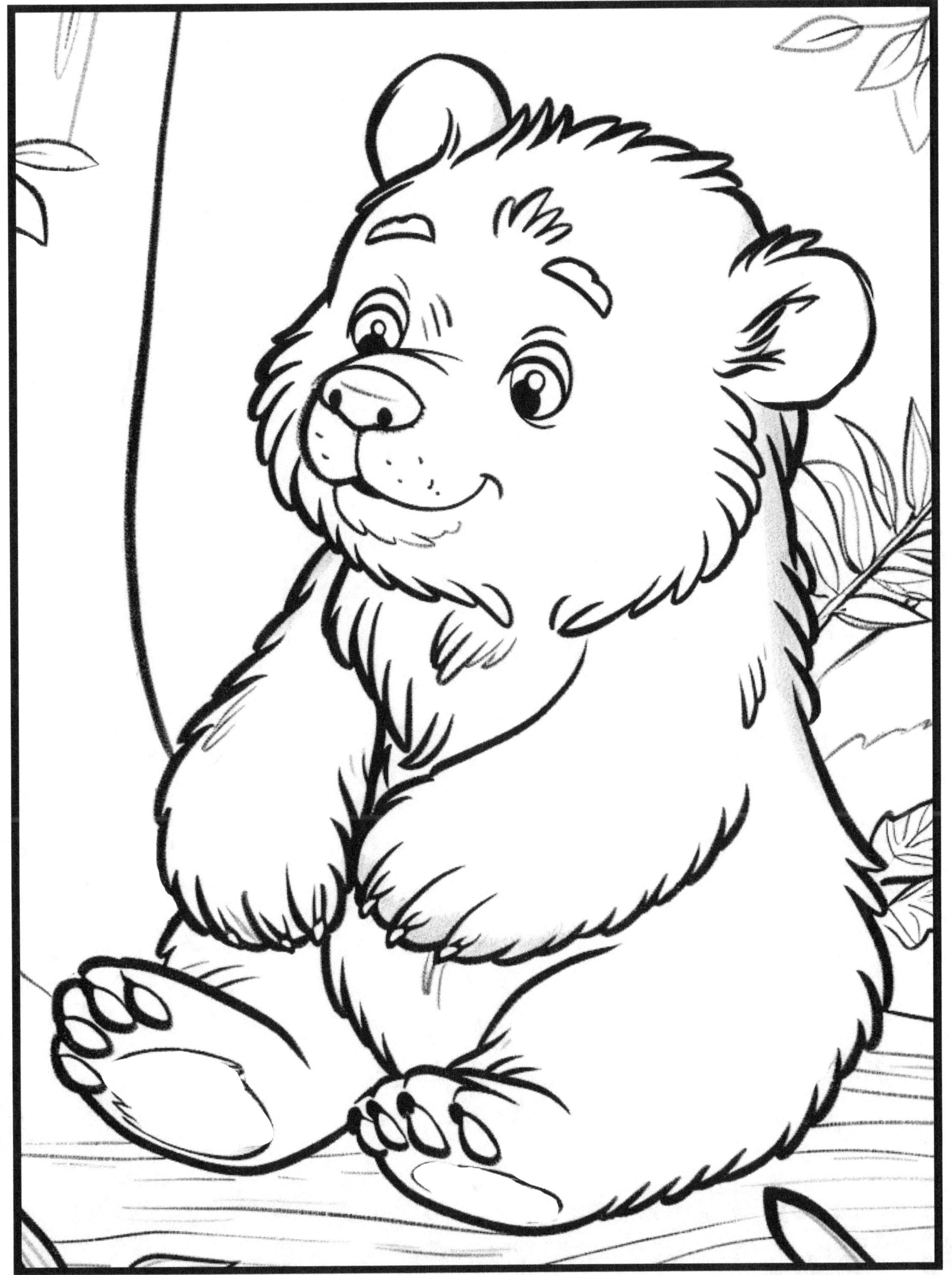